T0068141

HEALING ACROSS TIME III

PRAYERS FOR PROTECTION, CLEARING, AND HEALING

Lorrie Leigh

HEALING ACROSS TIME III
PRAYERS FOR PROTECTION, CLEARING, AND HEALING

iUniverse books may be ordered through booksellers or by contacting:

iUniverse
1663 Liberty Drive
Bloomington, IN 47403
www.iuniverse.com
844-349-9409

ISBN: 978-1-6632-5848-9 (sc)
ISBN: 978-1-6632-5849-6 (e)

Library of Congress Control Number: 2023922843

Print information available on the last page.

iUniverse rev. date: 11/29/2023

CONTENTS

SECTION III: CLEAR HOME, SELF, OTHERS, PLANTS, ANIMALS

PREFACE

I can say unequivocally that *Healing Across Time III: Prayers for Protection, Clearing, and Healing* originated in the Divine, in the Godhead.

This is the story: As I mentioned in the preface of *Healing Across Time I* and *Healing Across Time II)*, after having a profound spiritual experience in my mid-forties, I was strongly drawn to spend an hour each day reading the Bible and writing my thoughts and prayers about those passages.

A few months later, a friend received a message from the Holy Spirit that during my "quiet time," after spending a few minutes in prayer, I should write down the thoughts that come to mind.

That was the beginning of Spirit (Father God, the Holy Spirit, Jesus) leading me on a healing journey that I recount in *Healing Across Time I* and *Healing Across Time II*. Those two books contain most of the prayers and processes for protection, clearing, and healing that are in Healing Across Time *III*.

My Background and Experience with Prayer

I helped pray with people at the charismatic prayer group meetings I attended for eight years. Following the Holy Spirit's prompting, I prayed with a great many people through the years with gratifying results. I read a number of books about praying for clearing and healing.

I learned through personal experience the effects that negative energy (see Glossary) and the presence of Souls or entities that have negative energy can have on a person. In *Hat I* and *Hat II*, I tell about many of those experiences and the understandings I received from Spirit about how to do clearing and healing. I added that information in *Healing Across Time III* as I learned new things. I came to understand that the plan for my Soul was for me to have many experiences of needing clearing, so I would write about them for others to learn from.

Re Previous Lifetimes

I will include a quote from *Healing Across Time I:*

"Many of you reading this may not believe in people living more than one lifetime. I am not trying to convince anybody that that is the case. I am simply relating my experiences and what I learned from Spirit. Messages I received from Spirit regarding that:

> "Mar 1, '08. [| Only part of your Spirit is incarnated at any given time. The rest of your Spirit, your Higher Self, oversees your experiences and lovingly directs you from the spirit world. Your Higher Self is one with Me, yet distinct as a Spirit. |]
>
> "May 7, '08. Father God, does each portion of one's Full Soul live a human life only once? [| Y |] Since the Soul portions are from a unit, does it seem to each portion of the Soul like the experiences of the other portions happened to them? [| Y |] Does our Soul carry the memories of all our lifetimes? [| Y |]"
>
> (HAT I pp. xv, xvi)

A gentle suggestion for those who do not believe that people live more than one lifetime: There would be no harm in saying prayers and doing processes for yourself or others that refer to previous lifetimes. In case *that is the case* that you or they lived other lifetimes, you would have that base covered.

Things to Know

[| ... |] Portions enclosed in brackets are understandings and answers I received from Spirit (Father-Mother God, the Holy Spirit, Jesus).

(....) Means it is your choice who to address prayers to: Abba, Father God, Mother God, Lord, Jesus, Holy Spirit, Divine Love, Creator God, Yahweh, Jehovah, my Higher Power, or others.

Choices offered in some of the prayers are suggestions only, e.g., "...as a prayer for my family (for the salvation of Souls) (for peace in the world) (for healing for N__)." Please insert the intention(s) of your choice.

Based on my experiences with negative energies, outside Souls, and entities, I suggest a frequency for some prayers and processes. The suggested frequencies are noted in the Contents and in the text. You are free, of course, to make your own choices and timetable.

(SEE LIST) Means to check under that heading in the text.

(DO ONCE) One time should be sufficient for saying that prayer or making that declaration, but feel free to repeat it.

(2-4 Wks) (6-12 Mo) Feel free to say those prayers and (or) make those declarations more often.

Prayers and processes that do not have a frequency listed are there for when you need them and as suggestions for what to do and how to pray about a particular situation.

See the Glossary for definitions of words and phrases. Some of the meanings apply specifically to this writing.

Signing Off

This Trilogy of Books writing project has been my focus for the last thirty-plus years. I had a spiritual drive to continue on that I attribute to Spirit. I learned that completing this writing and getting *Healing Across Time I*, *Healing Across Time II*, and *Healing Across Time III* published is one of my Soul's primary purposes for this lifetime. Through inspiration from the Holy Spirit, the grace of God, and being buoyed up by encouragement from friends, that task is nearing completion.

Father-Mother God, Holy Spirit, Heart, I place this book in Your hands. Please draw those people to read it who are meant to. Protect and be with them as they pray for clearing and healing. Please spread the word in the spiritual realm that there is hope and that help is available.

Thank You for keeping Your promise:

"I will lead the blind by ways they have not known, along unfamiliar paths I will guide them; I will turn the darkness into

light before them and make the rough places smooth. These are the things I will do; I will not forsake them." (NIV Is 42:16).

May the explanations, prayers, and processes given in this book help many people learn how to stay protected, do clearing, and receive healing, and may their healing, in turn, help bring healing to their families, their communities, and our world.

Thank You, God, for hearing this prayer!

Signed with love,
Lorrie

ACKNOWLEDGEMENT

Thank You, Father-Mother God, Holy Spirit, and Jesus for Your love, teaching, and guidance throughout my life. Thank You for sustaining me in good health and "keeping faith in me."

Thank you, Fern, for being a loving, nonjudgmental friend, for joining me in receiving understandings from Spirit for eight years while you were still living and, since January 2010, being on the spiritual writing-editing team that has patiently assisted me with getting the writings into a suitable form for publishing. Thank you to every member of that team. God bless all of you!

Thank you, Beth Stein, for being a loving, nonjudgmental friend, offering encouragement, double-checking answers from the Holy Spirit, ministering to me, and being my spiritual sister. God bless you!

Thank you, Jennie Seil, for your love and encouragement and for being there for me. We met only a few years ago, but I immediately felt like we had known each other for a long time. God bless you!

SECTION I

INFORMATION AND PREPARATION

A. SIGNS OF NEEDING CLEARING, WHAT TO DO

The definition of negative energy for this writing:

"For each person, energy that has a lower vibration rate than their energy; energy that is lacking in positive character, such as anger or greed; energy that diminishes, deprives, or denies a person's energy; negative spirit." (Glossary)

The first steps to take to protect oneself from negative energies is not to associate with people who have a negative attitude towards others, life, etc., those who "don't sit right with you," and not to frequent places where you don't feel comfortable energy-wise or where people with negative energy are likely to gather, such as bars.

1. Negative Energy Can Cause

    a. Pain anywhere in your body, headaches (including migraine), backache, neuralgia, arthritis, digestive problems, "foggy" thinking, a feeling of pressure in your head, feeling very tired after watching a movie or program on TV, computer, or movie screen

    b. Problems with sleeping, having disturbing dreams

    c. Feelings of depression, anxiety, fear; feeling out of sorts, jittery

      Contact points for negative energy can cause the problems listed because they attract negative energy.

    d. Experiencing emotions that are unusual for you, such as anger or sadness. Those emotions might be those of outside Souls or entities that are with you. They

1

could also be repressed emotions of your own that are surfacing.

I experienced all of the above from a few to many times. The very low vibration energy level of unloving Souls causes the worst symptoms for those whose Soul is loving. I developed a bad headache and high blood pressure immediately after being near a person whose Soul was unloving or who had an unloving Soul with them. (I learned the cause later from the Holy Spirit.)

Most of the time, I felt better within 2 to 24 hours after doing a clearing for outside Souls and negative energies.

e. If a house or building was built on a burial site, energies from the Souls of people who are buried there may cause health or other problems for those who live or work in it. If problems are occurring, clear negative energies (III.B.1.a-d) and outside Souls (III.C.1.a-c) from the Souls of whoever is buried there and from the house or building itself (III.A.6, 9, or 14.e).

f. Electronic equipment to quit working

My printer quit working after someone with negative energies (I learned what caused it from the Holy Spirit later) used my computer and printer briefly. It took several attempts to clear the negative energy from the printer.

g. Plants not doing well (Some of my plants quit growing because of having Souls enmeshed with them. They resumed growing after I cleared out the Souls.)

2. Outside Souls Can Cause

a. All of the symptoms and problems listed in a-d above, because, most of the time, negative energies that are with a person are with or attached to one or more outside Souls that are with them. The ill effects are caused by the negative energies, not by the outside Souls themselves.

Experiencing problems or symptoms that a relative had (or has) can be a sign that their Soul is asking for help to get negative energy cleared from them.

b. Not being able to get your former spouse, lover, or friend out of your mind; feeling like they are still "with you," trying to control you. It is likely that a portion of their Soul is with you. (Clear outside Souls: III.C.1.a-d)

c. One to suddenly become very chilly. That can be a sign that an outside Soul is present.

d. The Soul might have come to ask for prayer for clearing or healing for themselves or a loved one or forgiveness for something in their current or previous lifetime. It could also be the Soul of a loved one visiting you.

Suggestions: In your own words, forgive them for whatever they are asking to be forgiven for. Clear negative energies (III.B.1.a-d) and outside Souls and entities (III.C.1.a-c) from that Soul and the people (Souls) it is concerned about.

e. Sounds as a signal that they are asking for help. I learned from the Holy Spirit that spirits of animals will sometimes cause sounds as a way of helping a Soul. A number of times, I heard the sound of a woodpecker coming from the dashboard of my car, rattling in the front doors of my car while I was driving, and muffled knocking coming from inside my bathroom floor. Twice, I heard a mouse scratching on the back of my bathroom mirror. In each case, the sounds quit after I helped the Soul (or Souls) asking for help. It sometimes took more than one clearing to free them.

3. Suggested First Clearings and Steps

Do the following clearings and steps one at a time. You may choose what order to do them in. Wait 4-5 days before doing the next one to see if the clearing that you did makes a difference in how you feel.

    a. Clear negative energies from yourself and the people you live with: III.B.1.a-d

    b. Clear outside Souls and entities from yourself and the people you live with: III.C.1.a-c

    c. Ask to have a protective valve placed in Soul ties and umbilical cords between you and others: II.B.9.a

    d. Dispose of items connected with former spouse(s), lover(s), and friends.

4. Indication of Needing a Specific Clearing

    a. Feeling like you are not alone.

       i. Separate Siamese twin Soul from your Soul: III.C.5

       ii. Clear Soul infestation: III.C.2.a-g

    b. Feeling like you are still connected with your mother

       Separate your mother's intergrafted Soul from your Soul: III.C.6

    c. Having personal and family relationship problems

       Go through a Process of Forgiveness *for past lifetimes* in person or in spirit with those with whom you have relationship problems: II.E

       If that doesn't help, go through a Process of Forgiveness in person or in spirit with those people *for both current and past lifetimes.*

5. Suggested Daily Prayers (Handy List)

    Besides saying the prayers listed below, I give myself a big hug in the morning and say, "I love you, Lorrie!" It gives a great start to the day. Try it!

    a. Prayer of Blessing: II.A.1

       "Bless me in who I am and in who I am coming to be!"

    b. Prayers for protection

       i. Set spiritual boundaries: II.B.1

         "At all times, only those loving Souls and entities who have permission from the Holy Spirit, my Higher

Self, may be with any part of me, with outside Souls that are with me, or in my (our) home or car, (or at my place of work). Only those Souls and entities with permission may approach me for help, prayer, or other reasons."

ii.   Protection for self, family, and home: See II.B.2

If you live alone: "(....), please seal the aura of every part of my Soul with Divine love and fill me, my home, and everything I own and use with Divine love. Thank You!"

If you live with family: "(....), please seal the aura of every part of my Soul, the aura of everyone in my (our) family, and everything we own and use, with Divine love. Thank You!"

iii. Holy Spirit demagnetizing shower: III.A.9

If you live alone: "(....), please flow a Holy Spirit demagnetizing shower through me, through all outside Souls and entities that are with me, and through my home (and car) to clear and transmute Soul residue and negative energies. Thank You!"

If you live with family: "(....), please flow a Holy Spirit demagnetizing shower through me, (my husband, wife), and everyone in my (our) family; through all outside Souls and entities that are with any of us; and through my (our) home and car to clear and transmute Soul residue and negative energies. Thank You!"

c.   Protection from negative energies from electronics: II.B.6.c

"(..., please place) (I place) a golden mesh of love over the speaker and receiver of my (our) telephone(s) and a spiritual firewall around all TVs, computers, and other electronic devices in my (our) home and car (and at work)."

  d. Ask for your food to be filled with Divine love: II.A.5

    "(....), please fill my food and drink, and everything that enters my body in other ways (makeup, ointments, injections) with Divine love. Thank You!"

B. QUESTIONS AND ANSWERS

1. Why pray for protection? Because one can so easily pick up negative energies.

  "Every living thing has its own vibration. Every inanimate object carries traces of the energy of those who made, sold and owned it. One can pick up negative vibrations by being around or touching someone or something that has a strong negative vibration." (Mickaharic pp. 6-7 adapted)

  Regularly asking for protection and doing clearing for oneself and one's surroundings is especially important for "sensitives" (empaths) who pick up energies very easily. (See Appendix C)

2. Should one ask permission before praying for people (Souls) for clearing or healing?

  Yes, but one does not need to ask permission in person. Before praying, say aloud or have the intention in mind that all prayers you say for others are dependent on each of those Souls being willing to have you pray for them. Parents have the authority to do clearing and healing for their minor children.

3. Does one need to ask permission before blessing people?

  No, because blessing someone is not a prayer for them to change in any way.

4. Is it acceptable to say the prayers in one's own words?

  Yes. You may also add additional prayers that come to mind. The steps and prayers are for guidance.

5. When praying for several people, can one say the prayers once and ask to have them applied to all those people?

    Yes. Before or after praying, say: "(....), please apply these prayers to N__ and N__ (to everyone in my family), also. Thank You!"

6. Is there a way for one's prayers to remain in effect longer?

    Yes. Say, "(...,) I ask for these prayers to remain in effect for a week (month, three months). Thank You!"

7. How does one arrange to have a Spiritual Ministry Team join them when they pray for somebody?

    If you have not done so, first ask for a Spiritual Ministry Team to be assigned to you (II.D.2), then say, "Ministry Team, please join me as I pray for (....)"

8. Can everyone be healed?

    Being healed or not depends upon several factors:

    a. The keys to effective prayer are intention, emotion (firm belief), and expectation. Both the person doing the praying and the person being prayed for need to fully want the healing to take place and firmly believe that it will.

    b. The Soul of the person being prayed for must choose for the healing to take place:

        "As some of you will evolve in your lives to be healers, let me remind you that there are some souls that do not wish to be healed. 'You must be healed,' is so often the message that is given with the healing.

        "No, they must not be healed. Only if they want to. And you are not the authority on that. Do not inflict your will. Just give love. The soul will take that love and put it where it can best be used." (Emmanuel's Book p. 166)

    c. Those unwilling to release negative energies will not be healed, e.g., unforgiveness, anger, judgment, lust.

    d. Those unwilling to give up the secondary gain they are receiving from being sick, crippled, or whatever will not be healed. (They may not realize they are "getting something out of" the situation.)

9. Is it OK to try to change the beliefs of a person who is near death?

No, it is advised against. A couple who were trained in palliative care told me they were taught that one should not try to change the beliefs of a person who is near death, because it would cause them to be anxious and unsettled.

Many websites give suggestions for caring for those who are near death, e.g., the National Institute of Aging.[1]

C. MESSAGES FROM SPIRIT RE PRAYERS

1. The Process of Forgiveness

Aug 4, '09. [| It is common to have relationship problems between people and between families. Troubles and mix-ups between individuals and families are often firmly rooted in past lifetimes. That is so much the usual thing that I will say that *such mix-ups are invariably rooted in past lifetimes.*

You do not need to know details about what experiences from past lifetimes are causing problems when those lifetimes occurred or who was related or connected to those problems in past lifetimes. I arranged to have many details uncovered about the interconnectedness of Souls in the Leigh family line as an example.

"Many topics need to be addressed through prayer if those praying for the healing of a family line are to be successful. There are steps that should be taken and things that should be expressed aloud so they will come to be.

One step I am speaking of is *for people with relationship problems to meet in person,* preferably in a neutral setting, with a neutral person on hand to act as a coordinator if you consider that necessary. While they are meeting, neither party may say anything about problems or issues connected with this lifetime. They are meeting only to clear up carry-over effects from earlier lifetimes. The steps I am giving just now apply only to earlier lifetimes. []

Father God then described the Process of Forgiveness.

2. Praying for One's Family Lines

    a. May 21, '10. [| It may seem to you that clearing will never be completed for any family line. You feel it is your responsibility to figure out how to clear the mess from everybody. Please back off and trust that all is well! Leave everything, yourself included, in My hands.

        For all you know, much of what you view as clearing that "needs to be done" may be experiences that those Souls chose to experience, or they may be "playing a part" to bring about healing for another person or persons. []

    b. Jun 9, '10. [| The best and most sensible approach to bringing clearing and healing to yourself or others is to do the various clearings one at a time. There is no hurry or pressure about any of them. Do a particular clearing when you feel drawn or inclined to do it with complete peacefulness. Having a period between doing the clearings is perfectly alright. []

    c. Mar 31 '12. It seems that what we in the family should do to bring about clearing and healing for every part of every person (Soul) in our family lines is to love every person (Soul) unconditionally, with no judging or categorizing whatsoever. [| Y |]

    d. Apr 17, '12. Do most people have portions of their Souls that need to be freed? [| Y |] Is that true for almost every lifetime for most people? [| Y |]

        To me, that indicates that everyone would benefit from doing most or all of the prayers and processes for clearing their family lines and their Soul line.

        [| Yes, for those who are sincere about wanting to be loving and to be cleared. |]

3. Praying for Clearing and Healing

    a. May 21, '10. [| Clearing, whether for an individual or a family line, is not simply a "done deal" when you complete the steps given for clearing. Prayer for ongoing clearing and healing is needed, especially when signs come up of further problems. |]

    b. Dec 12, '10. [| When someone allows negative energy to be within or somewhat attached to them, they have an immediate magnetic connection with that type of energy wherever it is. There are also weaker automatic connections with buddy energies that like to hang around with certain energies.

        The time will come when people will be well advised to clear their Souls as a treatment for physical problems. Some clinics may be opened that teach about the effects of negative energies on health and how to clear them. |]

    c. Dec 17, '12. [| Praying with emotion, with heartfelt feelings of love, and a strong wish for blessings, clearing, and healing for those you are praying for is the key to receiving the answers to your prayers. |]

    d. Jul 17, '21. [| What each person believes is perfect for them. It is the love within each and all that unites you. It is love that each person (Soul) is seeking. Every person is, so to speak, "shored in" by what they were taught, by the influence of other people and the world around them, by experiences they have had in this lifetime and previous lifetimes, and even by lessons they are meant to learn. |]

        Father, are You saying between the lines that it would be OK to pray for others according to their beliefs, to give encouragement and spiritual advice in those terms? [| You have the right idea. Ask the Holy Spirit to guide you. Even silently loving and blessing others exactly where and as they are ministers healing to them. Peace! |]

        Thank You, Father God!

D. PREPARATION FOR MINISTERING TO OTHERS

A person who wishes to do clearing and pray for healing for others on a regular basis must be of good moral character.

1. Do Thorough Clearing for Yourself
    a. Ask the Holy Spirit to place a protective valve in all soul ties and umbilical cord connections between you and other people and Souls: II.B.9
    b. Clear negative energies from yourself: III.B.1
    c. Go through a Process of Forgiveness in person or in spirit with those you have "unsettled situations" with.
    d. Go through a Process of Forgiveness in spirit with family members and your friends as a group: II.E.1.a-d
    e. Clear unhealthy enmeshments between you and others, living and deceased: III.C.1.b
    f. Clear outside Souls from yourself whose energy is detrimental to you: III.C.1.a-c
    g. Cancel detrimental vows you made in your current and previous lifetimes that are still in effect: III.F.5
    h. Clear curses still hanging over you related to your words or actions in this or earlier lifetimes: III.E.5

    If a situation should arise that you feel a need to pray for somebody immediately, first seal up all negative energies that may be with you or with that person:

    "(In the name of Jesus,) I seal all lower vibration (negative) energies that are with me and with N__ with spiritual lead. Jesus, Holy Spirit, please guide me. Thank You!"

2. When Ministering to Others
    a. Ask for clearing and protection for yourself, your home (the room you will minister in), those who will minister with you, and those you will minister to (II.B.2).
    b. If you wish, have quiet music playing while you are ministering.
    c. Ask your Ministry Team to join as you do the ministry.

    d. After the ministry, you and the person (people) you ministered to should each drink a glass of water.

    e. Thank the Ministry Team for their assistance. If you wish, ask them to continue ministering to the person (people) for another half hour (with music playing).

E. WORDS TO THE WISE

Things I learned from reading books about ministering to people, attending a charismatic prayer group for ten years, and personal experience:

1. For safety reasons, it is best for a woman not to be alone when ministering to somebody you do not know very well, especially when it is a man. An outside Soul (or spirit of negative energy) that is with the person may take over to try to prevent its being sent away. Some of them are very strong.

2. A person who has negative energy will attract negative energy, hence the importance of staying protected and doing clearing regularly.

    A common way for outside Souls and negative energies to transfer from one person to the next is through direct contact. So, if you do not know someone very well, it is wise to minister to them from within their aura, not by direct touch. This is especially important for those who pick up energy easily. I learned that lesson the hard way.

3. Do not minister to others when you are not feeling well, are very tired, or feel depressed or anxious.

4. Do not minister to someone if you feel a "check in your spirit," a gut feeling that you shouldn't do it. That type of feeling is one's intuition speaking. The Holy Spirit works through a person's intuition and common sense.

5. Do not minister to someone just because you feel you should. Let the Holy Spirit, your intuition, and common sense be your guide.

SECTION II

BLESS, PROTECT, HEAL, ASSIST, FORGIVE

A. PRAYERS OF BLESSING (DAILY: SEE LIST)

1. (DAILY) "Bless me in who I am and in who I am coming to be!"
2. "Bless you, N__, in who you are and in who you are coming to be!" (Blessing people (Souls) helps enable them to release negativity and choose good.)
3. "Bless each of you in my (our) family in who you are and in who you are coming to be!"
4. "Bless You, (....)! Bless you, Mother Earth! Bless you, Brother Sun! Bless you, Sister Moon! Bless all that is!"
5. The first time you eat for the day

   (DAILY) "(....), please fill my food and drink, and everything that enters my body in other ways (makeup, ointments, injections) with Divine love. Thank You!"

   Note: Food gets filled with Divine love when one says, "Bless this food."
6. Help others by offering the day as a prayer:

   (DAILY) "I offer all the events of today and everything that I think and do and say as a prayer for my family (for the salvation of Souls) (for peace in the world) (for healing for N__)."

B. PRAYERS FOR PROTECTION

1. Set Spiritual Boundaries (DAILY)

   "At all times, only those loving Souls and entities who have permission from the Holy Spirit, from my Higher Self, may be with any part of me, with outside Souls that are with

13

me, or in my (our) home or car, (or at my place of work). Only those Souls and entities with permission may approach me for help, prayer, or other reasons."

2. Protection for Self, Family, Home (DAILY, DO ONCE: SEE LIST)

   a. (DAILY) Seal aura, ask to be filled with Divine love

   If you live alone: "(...), please seal the aura of every part of my Soul with Divine love and fill me, my home, and everything I own and use with Divine love. Thank You!"

   If you live with family: "(....), please seal the aura of every part of my Soul, the aura of everyone in my (our) family, and everything we own and use, with Divine love. Thank You!"

   b. Protection for yourself

   "I invite Divine love to totally fill me. I ask for a shield of violet light in front and back of me and a cross of blue-white flame in front of my solar plexus. I visualize a circle and tube of blazing white Christ light around my aura and under my feet.

   "I call for a mirror-like substance around the outside so that anything of a negative nature that tries to touch it will be immediately reflected back to its source, and we send it back with Divine Love." (Starr pp. 10, 136, adapted)

   c. Live in an apartment or condo: Prevent negative energies from entering through floors and walls.

   (DO ONCE) "I seal the ceiling and floor, and the walls of my (our) apartment (condo) that adjoin other units, with spiritual lead, and place a spiritual firewall in them. (...), I ask for that protection to remain in place all the while I (we) live here. Thank you!"

3. Prayer of Protection – Unity

   "The love of God enfolds me.
   The power of God protects me.
   The presence of God watches over me.
   Wherever I am, God is!" (Freeman; Unity)

(Light, love, power, and presence are in alphabetical order.)

4. Protective Balloon

   Suitable for everyone. Picture a balloon around yourself that allows only beneficial energy to enter. Suggest that your children do that before entering a store, going to school, staying overnight with a friend, and so on.

5. Spiritual Armor, Angels for Protection (SENSITIVES DAILY)

   "(....), I ask for a helmet and full body armor of spiritual lead and for an army of angels to be with me for protection. Thank You!"

6. Protection Around Photos, Names, Electronics

   a. Photos (2-4 WKS)

      "(In the name of Jesus), I seal with Divine love all images of myself and those with me in photos of every format: printed and electronic. I ask for that protection to remain in place for a month."

   b. Names (SENSITIVES DAILY)

      "I seal my name with Divine love in all formats: in people's thoughts, spoken, printed, written, and electronic. Thank You, (...,) for that protection."

      "(....), please immediately seal everybody's name that I think of or say whose energy level is not beneficial for me. Thank You!"

   c. Electronics (DAILY)

      "I place a golden mesh of love over the speaker and receiver of my (our) telephone(s) and a spiritual firewall around all TVs, computers, and other electronic devices in my (our) home and car (and at work)."

7. Lessen Effects of Family Distress (SENSITIVES DAILY: SEE LIST)

   a. SENSITIVES DAILY: Pray the *Lord's Prayer* before one or more meals for family members and friends, both living and deceased, who are asking for prayer.

   b. Say *Prayer of Blessing* often for family members: II.A.3

    c. Go through a *Process of Forgiveness* in spirit between you and all living and deceased family members and between you and your friends: II.E

    d. Hold a memorial service by yourself or with one or more family members for all deceased family members who are asking for prayer and for aborted, miscarried babies of your own or family members. Name any babies that have not been named, such as those lost through miscarriage.

    e. Especially when not feeling well, it is good to say:

        "My Soul, please flow continuous blessings and love to all energies, outside Souls, and entities that are with me and to all Souls in the healing ring surrounding my Soul. Thank you!"

8. Protect Cells from Incorporation by Energies, Souls, Entities (2-4 WKS, SENSITIVES DAILY)

    "I declare that only my Soul may enter new cells as they form in my body. (....), please protect all cells in my body so that no negative energies, outside Souls, or entities can become incorporated within them. Thank You!"

    "I ask that this remain in effect for a week (month). Thank You!"

9. Protective Valve in Soul Ties, Umbilical Cords (2-4 WKS)

    a. Between you and other people (Souls)

        (2-4 WKS) "(Holy Spirit), please place a protective valve that allows only love to travel in each direction in all soul ties and spiritual umbilical cord connections between me and other people (Souls) and between me and my Souls from other lifetimes. Thank You!"

    b. Between you and objects

        "(Holy Spirit), please place a protective valve that allows only love to pass in each direction in all energy connections between me and items that I own or use now, that I owned or used in the past, and that I will own or use in the future. Please keep that protection in place until it is no longer needed. Thank You!"

10. Seal Holes in Soul Wall (2-4 Wᴋs)

"(....), please seal my Soul wall with a golden mesh of love. Thank You!"

C. MEDITATION, HEALING

1. Grounding Exercises

   These exercises will help clear your mind and recharge your energy. (Quotes: Browne p. 178)
   a. Cover Your Crown: "*...place one hand over the crown [top] of your head.*" (Thirty seconds to 1 minute)
   b. Focus on Your Feet: "*...place all of your awareness on the bottom of your feet. Pay attention to any sensations.*" (Thirty seconds to 1 minute)
   c. Follow Your Breath: "*Close your eyes and as you inhale, trace the air as it enters your nose and goes into your lungs. On the exhale, follow the air leaving your lungs and exiting your nose or mouth.*" (One to 10 minutes)

2. Meditation

   Sit quietly for 10 minutes or longer, paying attention to your breathing. It may help concentration to repeat a mantra with each breath, such as "Peace" or "Om."

3. Ask to Be Ministered to In a Healing Ring

   "(....), I ask for a healing ring around me (N__) and around every part of my (his, her) Soul from other lifetimes that needs healing. Thank You!"

   "(....), I ask for everybody in my (N__'s) family who needs healing and is willing for that to take place, to be ministered to in a healing ring. Thank You!"

4. Spirit of Healing Prayer

   "(....), I ask for a spirit of healing to hover over me (N___) and everyone in my (his, her) family, and for healing love to flow through all of us (them) all day and night (for a week, month). Thank You!"

5. Laying on of Hands

   Ask the person what they would like prayer for. Allow healing love to flow through you as you minister.

   a. For physical healing

      i. For yourself: Place your hands on or a few inches above the area of your body that needs healing. (2-5 minutes)

      ii. For others: Place your hands on or a few inches above the area of their body that needs healing OR place one hand in front of and the other behind the person directly on or a few inches above the area that needs healing. (2-5 minutes)

   b. For emotional healing

      i. Place your dominant hand on your (N___'s) forehead and the other at the base of your (his, her) skull. (2-5 minutes)

      ii. Place both hands on or a few inches away from yourself (N___), slightly below your (his, her) waistline. (2-5 minutes)

6. Restore Cells' Original Blueprint (DO ONCE)

   Pray once a day for seven days:

   "(....), please restore the perfect original blueprint for all of the cells in my (N___'s) body (heart, digestive system). Cells in my (his, her) body, please follow the directions the Holy Spirit gives you. Thank you!"

7. Clear Erroneous Early Imprinting (DO ONCE)

   Say out loud, choosing to believe what you are saying:
   "I am worthy of being loved because I come from love.

I *am* love. Father God, Mother God, the Holy Spirit, and Jesus love me! The universe loves me! They all say that I am a beloved child of God! I join them in saying and proclaiming that I am a beloved child of God! I receive their love, and I love me!"

D. SPIRITUAL ASSISTANCE

1. Ask for a New Gatekeeper

    Helps with disturbing dreams: "(....), I ask for a new gatekeeper. Thank You!"

2. Ask to Have a Spiritual Ministry Team Assigned (DO ONCE)

    "(....), please assign a Spiritual Ministry Team to me that I can call on to pray for me when I need ministry and to join me when I minister to others. I ask these to be on the team: (Choose 3 or 4: Jesus, Lord Melchizedek, Mighty Astrea; Archangels Michael, Gabriel, Raphael, Zadkiel; Saints N__ and N__), and family members that the Holy Spirit appoints. Thank You, Holy Spirit!"

3. Ask to Be Ministered to in Heaven Hospital

    "(....), I ask to be ministered to in Heaven Hospital to receive (help for depression, whatever) (healing for my heart, lungs, whatever) and for that ministry to continue as long as I need it. Thank You!"

    "(....), I ask for N__ to be ministered to in Heaven Hospital to receive (help for depression, whatever) (healing for his, her heart, lungs, whatever) and for that ministry to continue as long as I need it (he, she needs it). Thank You!"

4. Apply, Reapply Prayers

    a. Apply prayers to others:

        "(....), please apply the prayers I said for myself (N__) just now (last week) to N__ (to everyone in my family who needs healing) (to all my Souls from other

lifetimes) (to every person/Soul who is asking for help").
Thank You!"

b. Reapply prayers to yourself and (or) others:

"(....), please reapply the prayers for clearing and healing that I prayed for myself (for N___) yesterday (last week). Thank You!

5. Prayer to the Holy Spirit (2-4 WKS)

This prayer is good for overall clearing.

"Holy Spirit, please clear, cleanse, balance, attune, harmonize, and align me with the universal Christ white light, the green healing light, the purple transmuting light, and the golden light of grace.

"Within the Will of God and for my highest good, I ask that all disharmonic and dross energies be released, transmuted back to their original and perfect form, and returned to their proper dimension. I ask that I be stabilized and protected from all internal and external influences counter to my Soul's purpose. And for this blessing, I give thanks! I give thanks! I give thanks!" (Author Unknown)

6. Help for Chronic Illness, Phobias, Cellular Memories

For a child: *"...in addition to seeking qualified medical help, try quietly reassuring your sleeping child, 'You can let go of your past life now. It's over, and everything that hurt you in that life is gone forever. You were born into this new life safe and healthy and whole. You don't ever have to suffer from that other life again.'"*

For yourself: *"Dear God, whatever my spirit mind and my cell memory might be holding from a past life that is harmful to me in any way, please help me release it into the cleansing white light of the Holy Spirit."* (Browne pp. 106-107)

The Spirit of Healing Prayer would be of help, also: II.C.4

7. Help Alleviate Medical Problems

    a. Clear negative energies: III.B.1.a-d
Clear outside Souls that are not meant to be with you: III.C.1.a-c

    b. Each day for one to three weeks

        "(....), please protect every cell in my body so that no outside Souls or negative energies can become incorporated into them. Please seal all parts of me and any visiting Souls that feel spiteful towards me with spiritual lead. Thank You!"

    c. Say the "Bless You" prayer for all parts of yourself and all visiting Souls: II.A

    d. Smooth out relationship difficulties with your spouse, children, and others. You can do that in spirit at any age, such as when your child was young and a hurtful situation occurred.

    e. The Spirit of Healing Prayer would be of help, also: II.C.4

8. Help With Addiction

    Those who have studied the subject say that addiction can result from a person trying to escape from or deal with painful emotions. The problem is, though, that addiction itself triggers painful emotions: "...someone with addiction may be prone to feeling [a great deal of] shame, helplessness, sadness, fear and guilt..."[2]

    The following may help the addicted person:

    a. Clear negative energies from yourself (N___): III.B.1.a-d

    b. Clear outside Souls and entities from yourself (N___): III.C.1.a-c

        When people who are caught up in an addiction die, their Souls will often hang around people who have that addiction to pick up their energy and "get high."

    c. Ask for protection each day. Suggestion: II.B.1, 3, or 5

    d. Ask for help from (God, your Higher Power):

        For yourself: "(....), please help me with my addiction to alcohol (tobacco, painkillers, caffeine, drugs, sex, pornography, overeating, compulsive lying, compulsive shopping, gambling, exercise, gaming, social media). Please help me recognize and deal with the pain or other problems that trigger this addiction. If I am at the point where I need help, please help me admit that and give me the courage to go for help. Thank You!"

        For others: "(....), please help N__ with his (her) addiction to alcohol (tobacco, painkillers, caffeine, drugs, sex, pornography, overeating, compulsive lying, compulsive shopping, gambling, exercise, gaming, social media). Please help him (her) recognize and deal with the pain or other problems that trigger that addiction. If he (she) is at the point that he (she) needs help, please help him (her) admit that and give him (her) the courage to go for help. Thank You!"

9. Receive Healing While Sleeping

    [| (FATHER GOD) When you lie down to sleep, I bid that you think of Me and choose to receive My love all night long. You can receive healing and blessings while you sleep.[3] |]

10. Use of Water to Promote Restful Sleep

    Set a glass of water at the head of your child's (the person's) bed OR put 2-3 cups of water and a pinch of sea salt in a bowl and place it under the child's (person's) bed. The water will absorb negative energies during the night.

    Nobody should drink the water. In the morning, use your non-dominant hand to empty the water in the toilet and rinse the glass.

    Having water in the room is especially beneficial for older people and invalids. It helps to maintain their energy. You can purchase sea salt at natural food stores and some grocery stores. (Mickaharic pp. 28-31 adapted)

11. Healing Touch: Smooth Out Aura, Clear Negative Energies

The person being ministered to can stand, sit, or lie down. Use pillows to represent a person who isn't present.

Hold your hands from 1-6 inches away from the person as you minister to them. Move your hands "down and away from the body, utilizing either short or long connected strokes in a graceful, sweeping motion." (Hover-Kramer p. 111) Minister longer to areas that were injured or are sore, cold, or extra warm.

a. Clearing for the person's arms and legs:

Arms: Place your hands near the outside and inside of the person's upper arm. Sweep your hands slowly down their arm past the fingertips. After each sweep, shake your hands lightly to clear negative energies. 2x

Legs: If the person is sitting, ask them to lift their leg off the floor. Place your hands near the top and bottom of the upper part of the person's thigh. Sweep your hands slowly down the person's leg and past their toes, repositioning your hands as needed. After each sweep, shake your hands lightly. 2x

b. Clearing for the person's whole body:

Have the person stand in front of a chair should they need to sit down. Have them sit if they are too tall for you to reach above their head.

i. Standing in front, place your hands above the person's head and sweep them slowly down their sides to the floor. Shake your hands lightly.

ii. Standing at the person's side, place your hands above their head and sweep them slowly down the front and back of the person to the floor. Shake your hands lightly.

iii. Hold your hands above the person's head. Flow in love, peace, and healing energy. Pray silently or speak words of love, blessing, and encouragement as the Holy Spirit prompts. If you feel led, ask for an anointing for the person: "(....), please anoint N__ for what he (she) is meant to do.

After ministering, wash your hands and wrists to clear negative energies. Both you and the person you ministered to should drink 6-8 oz. of water.

Receive Healing Touch Ministry in Spirit

(Sit or lie down.) "Ministry Team, please minister healing touch to me." Imagine the Team ministering to you using the healing touch method. Thank them.

12. Ministry by Medical Assistance Team (MAT)

   a. Lie on your back, side, or stomach on a bed or couch with a warm cover. Have phone and electronic devices turned off and in a different room. Hold an amethyst crystal or place it next to you if one is available.

   b. Ask the MAT Team to minister to you:

   "Medical Assistance Team that includes Jesus and Archangel Raphael and his Angels of Healing, please minister to me for healing and clearing for (describe symptoms) and whatever other healing and clearing I need. Thank you!"

   Remain lying for about 30 minutes. It's OK if you fall asleep.

   c. Closing: "I close this session now. Thank you, Jesus, Archangel Raphael, your Angels of Healing, and everyone on the Team for ministering to me!" Take your time to stand up. Drink 6-8 oz. of water.

13. Full Body Prayer

   These steps are based on what came spontaneously to mind when I prayed in spirit for a friend who was gravely ill. Feel free to alter or add to the steps.

   a. Place pillows on a couch to represent N__. Stand (or sit) beside the couch as you minister.

b. Ask for spiritual assistance:

"(....), please protect N__ and me as I pray for him (her). My guardian angel, N__'s guardian angel, the 24 Archangels, Jesus, (Reiki Masters, Medical Assistance Team), and members of N__'s family and family lines, please join as I pray for him (her). Thank you!"

"(....), if it is not in the plan of N__'s Soul for him (her) to be healed physically, please apply the prayers to his (her) Soul. Thank You!"

c. Picture N__ in a cocoon formed of peace.

Say: "Crystalline white light of Christ, please gently enter the cocoon and fill N__'s body and etheric field with light and peace."

d. Sweep your arms over N__ several times from head to foot, flowing in blessing and healing energy. Hold your hands for about a minute over each area of his (her) body that you know about that is affected by illness, injury, or disease, flowing in love and healing energy from God. (If you wish) say over each area:

"Be healed in the name of Jesus."

e. Hold your hands above N__ and pray:

"(....), please clear the cancer (arthritis, diabetes, kidney problems, whatever) and all other problems that N__ has with the functioning of his (her) body and mind. Please flow healing love into him (her) to lessen any pain he (she) is experiencing.

f. Invite negative (low vibration) energies that are with N__ to transmute to loving energy:

"I flow a deluge of love and blessing to any negative energies that are with N__. I invite each bit of that energy to receive love and blessings and choose to become neutral or loving energy. Those bits that choose to do so are free to leave.

"In-God-We-Trust Angels, please come with your nets and carry all remaining negative energies that are with N__ to another dimension to be transmuted back to their original and perfect form. Thank you, angels!"

g. Ask for an easing of pain:

"(....), I ask that N__ will have no pain, or that it will be at a manageable level for him (her), for however long he (she) has left in this world and that when his (her) time was up, he (she) will have the blessing of leaving peacefully. Thank You!"

Play inspirational music for 30 to 45 minutes as a continuing ministry for N__.

h. Say "Thank you." Apply prayers to others in the family:

"Thank you, 24 Archangels, Jesus, members of N__ 's family and family lines, and everyone else who joined in praying for him (her). Please continue ministering to him (her) until the music finishes playing. Thank you!

"Thank You (...,) for hearing my prayers and those of others who joined in praying for N__. Please apply the prayers that were said for him (her) to everyone in his (her) family and family lines in every past, present, and future lifetime. Thank You!"

14. Soul Retrieval

a. Portions of your Soul from this lifetime

"Bless all of you separated portions of my Soul. I invite you to return to me. Angels, please guide them on their way. Thank You!

"Welcome to you portions of my Soul that returned just now! (....), please flow healing love through every part of me. Thank You!"

b. Portions of your Souls from other lifetimes

"Bless all of you Souls from other lifetimes of mine. I invite separated portions of those Souls to return to your Home Soul. Angels, please guide them on their way. Thank You!

"(....), please flow healing through those Souls. Thank You!"

15. Assist Souls to Go to the Light, Including Animals

Suggestion: Lovingly tell the deceased person they have died. They may not be aware that they have. Tell the

a. In one's home or outside

"I create a positive vortex here (motion to the spot) for you to go to the light (Mom), (Dad), (N__), if you haven't yet done so and wish to now.

"Angels and archangels, please gather around the vortex as a welcoming presence.

"(Mom), (Dad), (N__), I invite you and other Souls who have permission from the Holy Spirit to be here to go to light now. Bless you on your way!

"Jesus, angels, relatives, and friends, please meet (Mom), (Dad), (N__), and the other Souls and accompany them as they go to the light. Thank you!

"I now close the vortex. Thank You, (....)!"

b. In a church:

"I create a positive vortex (high above the altar) (in the middle of the church) to only be used for Souls to go to the light.

"Angels and archangels, please gather around the vortex as a welcoming presence.

"I invite those Souls who are ready to go to the light now.

"Jesus, angels, relatives, and friends, please meet the Souls and accompany them as they go to the light. Thank you!"

(After a few minutes) "I now close the vortex. All Souls that do not have permission from the Holy Spirit to stay must leave the church. Angels, please see to it that all Souls leave that do not have permission to stay. Thank you!"

16. Assist Unloving Souls to Become Loving

"Loving Souls in my (our) family lines and my Soul line, please join in flowing a deluge of blessings and love to all unloving Souls that are with me (N___). Thank you!

"Souls that are with me (N___) that are unloving because of painful circumstances during your life or not having received enough love, we flow a deluge of blessings and love to you. We invite you to receive the blessings and love and choose to become loving. Bless you!"

To clear unloving Souls from yourself (N___), follow the directions in III.C.1.a-c.

E. PROCESS OF FORGIVENESS

Going through a process of forgiveness will clear karma between you and other people (Souls). P1, P2: Persons 1, 2

1. Between You and Others in Person

    a. P1 "N___, choosing with my will and speaking for this lifetime and all previous lifetimes of mine, I am sorry for everything that I said, thought, did, or neglected to do that hurt you in any way. I am sorry for judging you and for placing curses, hexes, or wishes for evil against you and your family, whether without realizing it or on purpose. I retract and cancel all of them. Please forgive me."

    b. P2 "N___, choosing with my will and speaking for this lifetime and all previous lifetimes of mine, I forgive you for everything you said, thought, did, or neglected to do that hurt me in any way. I forgive you for any times you judged me or placed curses, hexes, or wishes for evil against my family and me."

    c. P1 "Thank you!"

    d. P2 "You are welcome."

    e. Switch P1 and P2 and repeat steps "a" through "d."

    f.   P1, P2 "(....), please heal me and everybody else who needs healing related to my having placed judgments, curses, hexes, and other wishes for evil against them during this lifetime and other lifetimes. Thank You!"

    g. P1, P2 Affirmation of Forgiveness: *"I forgive others, and I forgive myself. God forgives me, and I am free."*[4]

2. Between You and Others in Spirit

    a.   Invite the people (Souls) to take part.

    b. Follow the steps in E.1 above, switching chairs as you speak for yourself and the other people (Souls).

3. Between You and God

Forgive God in your own words for things you feel hurt about.

Ask God for forgiveness:

"(....), choosing with my will and speaking for this lifetime and all of my previous lifetimes, I am sorry for everything that I said, thought, did, or neglected to do that offended You and hurt other people or myself in any way, especially for any times that I judged You or placed curses, hexes or wishes for evil against You, against people and myself. Please forgive me. Thank You!"

4. Forgive Yourself

Use your own words or the following:

"Choosing with my will and speaking for this lifetime and all previous lifetimes, I forgive myself for everything I said, thought, did, or neglected to do that hurt other people or myself in any way, especially for any times I placed judgments, curses, hexes or wishes for evil against God, other people or myself. I retract all of those ill wishes."

5. Between You and All Other People (Souls) (6-12 Mo)

"Every person and Soul this applies to, choosing with my will, speaking for this lifetime and all of my previous lifetimes, I am sorry for any times that I judged you and placed a hex, curse, or other wish for evil against you, whether without realizing it or on purpose. I retract all those judgments, hexes, curses, and wishes for evil and ask you to forgive me. Thank you!"

"Every person and Soul that the above applies to, I invite you to say, 'I forgive you.'"

"Thank you, everybody! God bless you!"

SECTION III
CLEAR HOME, SELF, OTHERS, PLANTS, ANIMALS

A. CLEAR OBJECTS, HOME, BUILDINGS

1. Clear By Command

   "(In the name of Jesus), I seal with spiritual lead all Souls and energies that are within or attached to this (object) or anywhere in my (our) home that are not beneficial for me (and my family). (In the name of Jesus), I ask kindly and command all of those Souls and energies to leave. (Cough)

   "Guardian angels of those Souls, please guide them to where they are meant to be. Thank you!

   "Holy Spirit, please transmute those negative energies back to their original and perfect form and return them to their proper dimension. Thank You! And please fill this (object), my (our) home, and everything I (we) own and use with Divine love. Thank You!"

2. Wash the Items.

3. Place the Items in Sunlight for 24 Hours

4. Bathe With Light

   "Visualize bright white light flowing over and around the object. Say: 'I surround and fill this object (building, area) with the light of Christ and release any negativity it might be holding. Thank You!'" (Browne p. 170, adapted)

5. Clear by Using a Copper Ring, Actual or Spiritual

   Create a spiritual copper ring: Motion to the selected location and say, "I place a spiritual copper ring here."

A spiritual copper ring dissolves within 24 hours,`` so you must create a new one each day to continue clearing whatever you had placed in it. To dissolve a spiritual copper ring before that, motion to its location and say, "I now dissolve this spiritual copper ring."

   a.   Box springs and mattress: Do not sleep on them during the clearing. For 24 hours each, place a copper ring (1) under them, (2) on top of them, (3) between them.

   b.   Bed, ongoing clearing: Place a copper ring on or under the bed during the day. Remove it before going to sleep (higher energy from it might keep you awake).

   c.   Furniture, larger appliances, cupboards: Place a copper ring on top or under for 24 hrs.

   d.   Objects, clothing: Place in a copper ring for 24 hours (36-48 hours if particularly negative energies might be attached to the objects or clothing).

   e.   Yourself: Stand in a copper ring for a few minutes, or place a copper ring under your chair for 15 minutes to an hour.

   f.   Food, Supplements, Baking Supplies: Place a copper ring on top of your refrigerator and freezer and above all cupboards and areas where those items are stored.

6. Lighted Candle, Holy Water

   Clear negative energies from one's home or a building: Carry a lit white candle into each room. Sprinkle each room with holy water and trace a sign (symbol) of your faith, such as a cross, with your hand. In each room, say:

   "Father God, please cleanse and purify this room with the white light of the Holy Spirit and fill it with Your loving grace. Thank You!" (Browne p. 178)

   Make Holy Water

   a.   Place water in a container and say: "(....), please fill this water with Divine love. Thank You!"

   b.   *"Let ordinary water sit in direct sunlight for three hours, and three times during those three hours, make any sign over it that has spiritual meaning and power for you. I, for example, make the sign of the cross."* (Browne p. 178)

7. Bowl of Water, Ice Cubes

Reduce the intensity of the emotional energy resulting from an argument *"by putting a bowl of water in the room where it is taking place or ice cubes on the floor, either while the argument is going on or as soon as it's finished."* (Mickaharic p. 76)

8. Clear By Use of Imagination

"The instant negative thoughts about yourself enter your mind...reach up to your forehead...picture an 'eject' button there. Push that eject button [and say,] 'I refuse this tape [and]...release its negativity from my mind into the white light of the Holy Spirit.'" (Browne p. 201)

9. Holy Spirit Demagnetizing Shower (DAILY)

If you live alone: "(....), please flow a Holy Spirit demagnetizing shower through me, through all outside Souls that are with me, and through my home (and car) to clear and transmute Soul residue and negative energies. Thank You!"

If you live with family: "(....), please flow a Holy Spirit demagnetizing shower through me, (my husband/wife), and everyone in my (our) family; through all outside Souls that are with any of us; and through my (our) home and car to clear and transmute Soul residue and negative energies. Thank You!"

10. Holy Spirit Vacuuming
   a. For Others

Standing behind the person, place your hands on the top of their head with your thumbs outstretched and your thumbs and middle fingers touching, forming a circle. Say, "Holy Spirit, please suction negative debris out of N__ beginning at the top of his (her) head and working downward."

After 5 minutes: "Now, please fill all empty places within N__ with sparkly-white, spiritual goo (love). Thank You, Holy Spirit!"

b. For Yourself

"Holy Spirit, please do spiritual vacuuming for me to clear negative debris, beginning at the top of my head and working downward."

After 5 minutes: "Please fill all empty places within me with sparkly-white, spiritual goo (love). Thank You, Holy Spirit!"

11. Meditate for Several Minutes

Sit quietly, breathing in through your nose and out through your mouth. Breathe in peace and love. Breathe out anxiety, fear, anger, and other negative energies.

12. Send Negative Energies into a Negative Vortex

"I create a negative vortex (outside by __). Angels, please protect that vortex and allow it to be used only to clear negative energies.

"I send all Soul residue and negative energies that are with me, with members of my (our) family, and in my (our) home into that negative vortex to be transmuted to neutral energy. (Pause) I now close the vortex. Thank you, angels, for your help!"

13. Clear Caffeine Energies from Self and Nearby Souls

Souls that crave the energies of caffeine hang around people who drink caffeinated beverages to absorb caffeine energies from them, thus possibly increasing those people's craving for caffeine. It is nearly impossible for Souls on the other side to do clearing for themselves, but you can ask for clearing of caffeine energies for them and yourself. Asking for this clearing will help those who wish to reduce or quit caffeine use entirely.

"(....), beginning now and continuing for three days and nights, I ask for the light of the Holy Spirit to flow through and around me and through and around Souls hanging around me to clear built-up caffeine energies. Thank You!"

14. Other Methods of Clearing Home, Spaces (DAILY: SEE LIST)

(DAILY) (Often): Do one or more of these:
a. Have crystals in the room
b. Play music (not rock or hard rock)
c. Have live plants in the home, room
d. Have a water fountain operating
e. Open windows and doors. Ask for the wind of the Holy Spirit to blow through to clear negative energies.
f. Smudge the objects and rooms with smoldering sage

B. CLEAR NEGATIVE ENERGIES FROM SELF, OTHERS

Why outside Souls (Soul portions) are with a person:

Energy level: Outside Souls are drawn to the person because the person's energy level is the same as those Souls. Clearing negative energies from oneself will prevent Souls with negative energies from being drawn to you.

To get help: Souls from previous lifetimes of one's own or Souls of family members or friends may come to a person to get help with getting negative energies cleared from them and (or) the enmeshment cleared between their Soul and your Soul, or between their Soul and one or more other Souls. If you send those Souls away without being helped, they will likely return and try again.

The following clearing includes clearing negative energies from outside Souls that are with a person and clearing enmeshment between those Souls and other Souls.

1. Steps in Clearing (2-4 Wᴋs a-c)
   a. Clear Incorporation of Negative Energies Retroactively
      (This will also clear outside Souls. Skip if you did this clearing within the last month.)

      If doing the clearing for another person, first say, "N___, please join in spirit."

      "I declare that only my Soul may enter new cells as they form in my body, and I apply that declaration retroactively as though I said it in my spirit every day since my conception.

      "Thank You (...,) for protecting all of the cells of my body all that while so no outside Souls or negative energies could become incorporated within them."
   b. Clear Enmeshment Between Negative Energies and Outside Souls and Entities

      "(In the name of Jesus), I ask kindly and command each bit of negative energy that is with outside Souls and entities that are with me (N___) to release to each of those Souls and entities every portion of their being that is enmeshed with your energy. Thank you!

      "Outside Souls and entities that are with me (N___), please release every bit of negative energy that is enmeshed with your being back to the energy body it is a part of. Thank you!"
   c. Clear Enmeshment Between Negative Energies and Your (N___'s) Soul

      "(In the name of Jesus), I ask kindly and command each bit of negative energy that is with me (N___) to release to me (him, her) every portion of my (his, her) Soul that is enmeshed with your energy. Thank you!

      "(N___, please join in spirit:) 'I release every bit of negative energy that is enmeshed with my Soul back to the energy body it is a part of.'"

    d. Command the Negative Energies to Leave

"I bless all energies that are with me (N__). Any bit of that energy that chooses to become loving or neutral energy is now free to leave. Go in peace!

"(In the name of Jesus), I ask kindly and command all negative energies that are still with me (N__) to leave. (Cough)

"Holy Spirit, please transmute those negative energies back to their original form and return them to their proper dimension. Thank You!"

    e. If Negative Energies Have Not Been Cleared

      i. Do a *Process of Forgiveness* in spirit with everyone, living and on the other side, where there is a need for it: II.E

      ii. *Cut detrimental soul ties* between you and others: III.B.1 Ask to have a *protective valve* placed in all Soul ties between you and others: II.B.9

      iii. Make the declaration: *Protect Cells from Incorporation by Souls, Energies* (II.B.8) every morning for nine days. At the end of the nine days, repeat steps a-c above.

      iv. Ask for ongoing clearing:

"(...,) I give You ongoing permission to command those energies to leave whose energy level is not beneficial for me. Thank You!"

Note: If it has been more than a month since you did clearing for negative energies (III.B.1.b-d), it is best to do so before doing a clearing for outside Souls.

C. CLEAR OUTSIDE SOULS AND ENTITIES

[Important: See the note above.]

1. Steps in Clearing: (2-4 WKS a-c)

   a. Clear Soul Incorporation Retroactively

      "I declare that only my Soul may enter new cells as they form in my body, and I apply that declaration retroactively as though I said it in my spirit every day since my conception.

      "Thank You (....,) for protecting all of the cells in my body all that while so that no outside Souls or negative energies could become incorporated within them."

   b. Clear Soul Enmeshment

      "Outside Souls that are not meant to be with me (N__) at this time, please release to me (him, her) all portions of my (his, her) Soul that are enmeshed with your Soul. Thank you!

      "Parts of me (N__), please join in saying, 'I release to each of you outside Souls all portions of your Soul that are enmeshed with my Soul that are not meant to be with me at this time.'"

      "By the sword of the Spirit, I declare that all enmeshments between my (N__'s) Soul and outside Souls that are not meant to be with me (him, her) at this time are cleared. Thank You (God, Spirit)!"

   c. Command Outside Souls to Leave

      "(In the name of Jesus,) I ask kindly and command all outside Souls to leave that are not meant to be with me (N__) at this time. (Cough) Thank you!"

      "Angels, please guide those Souls to where they are meant to be. Thank you!"

   d. If Unwanted Outside Souls Have Not Been Cleared

      i. *Do a Process of Forgiveness* in spirit with everyone, living and on the other side, where needed. Anger and ill will directed towards others create ties.

    ii. *Clear Soul Incorporation by the Nine-Day Process* (see below), then repeat steps II.C.1.b-c above.

    iii. Ask for ongoing clearing: "(...,) I give You permission at any and all times to direct outside Souls to leave whose energy level is not beneficial for me. Thank You!"

  e. Clear Soul Incorporation by Nine-Day Process

    Day 1: "Souls that are incorporated within cells of my body, I will do a nine-day clearing starting today that will gradually release those incorporated portions of your Soul so they can return to you. You will be. safe."

    Day 1 through 9: "I declare that only my Soul may enter new cells as my body forms them. (....), please protect all of the cells in my body so that no outside Souls or energies incorporate into them. Thank You!"

    Day 9: "Soul portions that were incorporated within cells of my body, I release to you every portion of your Soul that is enmeshed with my Soul. Please release to me every portion of my Soul that is enmeshed with your Soul. Thank you!" (Do steps II.C.1.b-c)

2. Clear Infestation from Your (N__'s) Soul (Do ONCE)

  a. If doing the clearing for somebody else, tell them in person or in spirit what you will be doing a clearing for:

    "N__, from what you described, an outside Soul and (or) negative energies may have intermingled with your Soul at the time of your conception or shortly afterward. Such intermingling at the time of conception is called Soul infestation.

    "I will be doing a clearing for you for Soul infestation and for infestation of negative energies that will include clearing for outside Souls that are with you without permission and for negative energies. The clearing should be complete within ten days."

b. Pray for clearing and protection for your (N___'s) Soul at conception

"Holy Spirit, please clear all negative energies from my (N___'s) Soul at the time of my (his, her) conception and place a protective shield around it. Thank You!"

c. Explain to the Soul that entered as an infestation what you will be doing

"Outside Soul that has been with me (N___) my (his, her) whole life, you are not meant to be with me (him, her). It appears that you joined with my (his, her) Soul at the time of my (his, her) conception or shortly after.

"This is my (N___'s) body, not yours. I will be doing a clearing to release your Soul. In about a week, you will be able to leave freely."

d. Say several times a day for seven days:

"Soul that is intermingled with my (N___'s) Soul, I flow a deluge of blessings and love to you. Bless you in who you are and in who you are coming to be!"

e. Clear incorporation of that outside Soul and negative energies from within cells of your (N___'s) body:

Aloud: "I declare that only my (N___'s) Soul may enter new cells as they form in my (his, her) body, and I apply that declaration retroactively as though I (he, she) said it in my (his, her) spirit every day since my (his, her) conception.

"Thank You, (....), for protecting all of the cells in my (N___'s) body since the time of my (his, her) conception so that no outside Souls and negative energies could become incorporated into them."

f. Clear enmeshment between that outside Soul and your (N___'s) Soul and command it to leave

"Outside Souls that are not meant to be with me (N___), please release to me (him, her) all portions of my (his, her) Soul that are enmeshed with your Soul. Thank you!

"N__, please join in spirit. 'I release to each of you outside Souls all portions of your Soul that are enmeshed with my Soul that are not meant to be with me.'"

"By the sword of the Spirit, I declare that all enmeshments between my (N__'s) Soul and outside Souls that are not meant to be with me (him, her) are cleared. Thank You, (....)!"

"(In the name of Jesus), I ask kindly and command all outside Souls that are not meant to be with me (N__) to leave! (Cough) Thank you!

"Angels and guides, please guide those Souls to where they are meant to be. Thank you!

g. Clear enmeshment between those negative energies and your (N_'s) Soul and command the negative energies to leave:

"I command each bit of negative energy that is with me (N__) or attached to my (his, her) aura to release to me (him, her) all portions of my (his, her) Soul that are enmeshed with its energy. Thank you!

"I bless all energies that are with me (N__). Any bit of that energy that chooses to become loving or neutral energy is now free to leave. Go in peace!

"(In the name of Jesus), I ask kindly and command all remaining negative energies to leave. (Cough)

"Holy Spirit, please transmute those lower vibration (negative) energies back to their original form and return them to their proper dimension. Thank You!"

3. Clear Lying Spirits, Mischievous Spirits

"(Holy Spirit), if any lying spirits are present, please turn their orientation to point to the truth. Thank You!

"I seal any lying spirits, poltergeists, and mischievous spirits that are present with spiritual lead and {in the name of Jesus) command them to leave!" (Cough)

4. Clear Supraphysical Shells (6-12 Mo)

    a. Say the following prayers for three to seven days

        Morning: "(....), I ask for Divine love to flow through me all day and night. I send love and blessings to the Souls that supraphysical shells that are with me are a part of. I ask for a *Compress of Spiritual Vinegar* and *Balm of Gilead* to remain in place all day around those shells. Thank You!"

        Evening: "(....), I ask for my Soul and all supraphysical shells attached to it to be immersed in a *Love Bath of Golden Saffron* all through the night. Thank You!"

    b. Call on Angels of the Violet Flame

        "Angels of the Violet Flame, please sweep violet transmuting light through all supraphysical shells that are attached to my (N__'s) etheric body to dissolve them and transmute that energy into light. Thank you, angels!" (Starr pp. 102, 103, adapted)

5. Separate Siamese Twin Soul from Your (N__'s) Soul (DO ONCE)

    It is OK to do this process even if you aren't sure that you (N__) had a twin.

    a. Address the Soul of your (N__'s) twin:

        "Soul of my (N__'s) twin that has been with me (him, her) since my (his, her) conception, you may feel like my (his, her) body is your body, but it isn't. It is my (N__'s) body.

        "I will ask the Medical Assistance Team to clear any soul essence that is connecting your Soul with my (N__'s) Soul so you and I (he, she) will both be individual Souls the way we are meant to be. There is nothing to be afraid of."

b. Ask the Medical Assistance Team to do spiritual surgery (Wright, throughout the book)

    i. For yourself: Lie down, then say:

"Medical Assistance Team, there are indications that the Soul of my twin has been with me for my whole life. If there is Soul essence connecting my twin's Soul with my Soul, please do spiritual surgery to separate them and ask for healing for all affected areas for both Souls. Thank you!"

Remain lying for 15 minutes, then say: "Thank you, Jesus, Archangel Raphael, your Angels of Healing, and the others on the Medical Assistance Team for ministering to me! Bless you!"

Take your time to sit and stand up. Drink 6-8 oz. of water.

    ii. For another person

If you are not with the person, arrange a time when they can lie down for 15 minutes while you do the clearing. Tell them to take their time afterward to stand up and to drink 6-8 oz. of water.

"Medical Assistance Team, there are indications that the Soul of N__'s twin has been with him (her) for his (her) whole life. If there is Soul essence connecting N__'s twin's Soul with his (her) Soul, please do spiritual surgery to separate the two Souls and ask for healing for all affected areas for both Souls. Thank you!"

At the end of 15 minutes, say: "Thank you, Jesus, Archangel Raphael, your Angels of Healing, and the others on the Medical Assistance Team for ministering to N__."

     c. Clear the incorporation of the Siamese twin Soul from within cells in your (N___'s) body: III.C.1.a

     d. Clear enmeshment between the Siamese twin Soul and your (N___'s) Soul and command the Siamese twin Soul to leave: III.C.1.b-c

6. Separate Mother's Intergrafted Soul from Your (N___'s) Soul (DO ONCE)

     a. Address your mother's Soul:

> "Mom, there are signs that your Soul and my Soul may have become somewhat connected before I was born. If a mother is very protective of herself out of fear, that protectiveness can extend to and into her baby and somewhat 'glue' the baby's Soul to her Soul. I will do a clearing to separate your Soul from my Soul if that is how things are. If not, there is no harm done."

     b. Clear the incorporation of your mother's Soul from within cells of your body: III.C.1.a

     c. Clear the enmeshment between your mother's Soul and yours; command her Soul to leave: III.C.1.b-c

D. CLEARING FOR PLANTS, ANIMALS

1. Clearing for Plants

     a. Clear negative energies from a plant

> "Each bit of negative energy within this plant or with Souls that are enmeshed with it, I ask kindly and command you to release every portion of the plant's spirit and every portion of those Souls that is enmeshed with your energy. Thank you!

> "Dear plant, please release every bit of negative energy that is enmeshed with your spirit back to the energy body it is a part of. Outside Souls that are with the plant, please release every bit of negative energy

that is enmeshed with your Soul back to the energy body it is a part of. Thank you!

"I bless all energies that are with this plant and with Souls that are enmeshed with it. Any bit of that energy that chooses to become loving or neutral energy is now free to leave. Go in peace!

"I command all negative energies that are still with this plant and that are with Souls that are enmeshed with the plant to leave. (Cough)

"Holy Spirit, please transmute those negative energies back to their original form and return them to their proper dimension. Thank You!"

   b. Clear Souls that are enmeshed with the plant

"Souls that are enmeshed with this plant, this is not the right place for you to be. Please release to it every portion of its spirit that is enmeshed with your Soul. Thank you!

"Dear plant, please release every portion of the Souls that are enmeshed with your spirit back to each of them. Thank you!

"Angels, please be on hand to guide the Souls that are with this plant to where they are meant to be. Thank you!

"All Souls that are with this plant, I ask you kindly and command you to leave. (Cough) Thank you!"

"(....,) please flow healing love through this plant so it can be restored to full health. Thank You!"

  2. Clearing for Animals

    a. Clear Soul incorporation

A__: The animal's name or "This Animal."

"Speaking for and with A__, I declare that only his (her, its) soul may enter new cells as they form in his (her, its) body, and I apply that declaration retroactively as though A___ said it in his (her, its) spirit every day of its life.

"Thank You (...,) for protecting all of the cells in A___ 's body all that while so that no outside Souls or negative energies could become incorporated within them."

b. Clear Soul enmeshment

"Outside Souls that are not meant to be with A___ at this time, please release to him (her, it) all portions of his (her, its) soul that are enmeshed with your Soul. Thank you!

"Dear A___, please join in spirit: 'I release to each outside Soul that is not meant to with me, all portions of its Soul that are enmeshed with my soul.'

"Angels, please be on hand to guide the Souls that will be leaving A___ to where they are meant to be. Thank you!

"Souls that are not meant to be with A___, I ask you kindly and command you to leave. (Cough) Thank you!"

"(...,) please flow healing love through A___ so he (she, it) can be restored to full health. Thank You!"

E. TARGETED CLEARING FOR NEGATIVE ENERGIES

1. Clear Energies of Allergies, Diseases, Infections

a. Write the names of the allergies, diseases, and other medical conditions affecting you (N___) and members of your (his, her) family on slips of paper. On another slip, write, "All other allergies, diseases, and medical conditions."

b. Create a positive vortex:

Motion to the selected spot and say: "I create a positive vortex here to be used only for releasing the energies of allergies, diseases, and other medical conditions from me (N___) and members of my (his, her) family. I ask angels to protect the vortex. Thank you, angels!"

    c. Place the slips in the positive vortex, then say:

"(In the name of Jesus), I clear the energies of these allergies, diseases, and medical conditions that have been affecting me (N___) and members of my (his, her) family. I send them back to where they came from to be transmuted to their original and perfect form. Thank You, (...,) for that clearing!"

    d. After doing the above steps, you (N___) should do this:

Say a *Prayer of Blessing* (II.A.1-3) and the *Spirit of Healing Prayer* (II.C.4) daily for ten days for yourself and those in your family who have or had the allergies, diseases, and (or) other medical conditions that you did the clearing for.

2. Clear Contact Points for Negative Energies (2-4 WKS)

"(....), please flow a Holy Spirit demagnetizing shower through me (N___) and my (his, her) home and car to clear any contact points for negative energies that are present. Thank You, Holy Spirit!"

3. Clear Negative Thoughtforms (6-12 MO)

    a. Clear astral connections between the makers of the thoughtforms and the Souls caught within them:

"Angels of the Violet Flame, please sweep violet transmuting flame through all negative thoughtforms that are attached to or hanging over me (N___) and members of my (his, her) family to dissolve the astral cords connecting the makers of those thoughtforms with Souls and to dissolve the thoughtforms, transmute their energy, and release the energy to be used for good. Thank you, angels!" (Starr pp. 66, 98)

    b. Clear enmeshment between the Souls and energies that are in the thoughtforms:

"I seal with spiritual lead all negative energies that are in negative thoughtforms that are hanging over me (N___) and members of my (his, her) family.

"(....), please flow a Holy Spirit demagnetizing shower through those negative thoughtforms to clear stickiness so Soul portions caught in them can easily separate from the negative energies. Thank You!

"(in the name of Jesus), I ask and command, the negative energies in the negative thoughtforms to release all Soul portions that are enmeshed with your energy. Thank you!

"All Soul portions caught in the negative thoughtforms that are willing to do so, please join in saying: 'I release all negative energies and all portions of other Souls that are enmeshed with my Soul that are not meant to be with me.'

"By the sword of the Spirit, I declare that all Soul portions in the negative thoughtforms that are hanging over me (N___) and my (his, her) family and family lines who chose to do so are separated from the negative energies and each other."

c. Command the negative energies to leave:

"I bless all energies that are with me (N___). Any bit of that energy that chooses to become loving or neutral energy is now free to leave. Go in peace!

"(In the name of Jesus), I ask kindly and command all remaining negative energies to leave. (Cough)

"Holy Spirit, please transmute those lower vibration (negative) energies back to their original form and return them to their proper dimension. Thank You!"

4. Clear Dark Energy Centers

We suggest to do this clearing if other prayers and processes you have tried don't seem to be helping.

a. Preparation: You (N___) pray once a day for three days

"My Full Soul and loving Souls in my (N___'s) family lines, please join me (him, her) in sending a steady barrage of blessings and love to all dark energy centers that are beaming dark energies at individuals, Souls and families in our family lines:

"'I ask for love and blessings to flow at every past and present moment to the compressed Soul portions that are being held captive in the dark energy centers, to the Souls and entities who are operating those centers, and to the dark energies themselves.

"(....), I ask that a Holy Spirit demagnetizing shower has been flowing along all the pathways that those dark energies traveled on ever since they were set up. Thank You!'"

   b. Clear enmeshment between Souls, negative energies

"I seal all negative energies that are in the dark energy centers that are hanging over me (N__) and members of my (his, her) family with spiritual lead.

"(....), I ask for a Holy Spirit demagnetizing shower to flow through those dark energy centers to clear stickiness so Soul portions that are caught in them can separate from the negative energies more easily. Thank You!

"(in the name of Jesus), I ask and command the negative energies in the dark energy centers to release all Soul portions that are enmeshed with their energy.

"All Soul portions caught in the dark energy centers that are willing to do so, please join in saying: 'I release all negative energies and all portions of other Souls that are enmeshed with my Soul that are not meant to be with me.'

"By the sword of the Spirit, I declare that all Soul portions in the negative thoughtforms that are hanging over me (N__) and over my (his, her) family and family lines who chose to do so are separated from the negative energies and each other. Those Soul portions who wish to are now free to leave."

5. Clear Curses, Hypnotic Suggestion, and Implants (6-12 Mo)

    a. Dissolve the roots of the curses and hexes:

"Loving Souls in my family and family lines, please join in sending a barrage of blessings and love to every person, Soul, and entity who took part in placing curses, hexes, and other wishes for evil against me and members of my family and family lines.

"I ask that ever since those curses, hexes, and wishes for evil were put in place, a Holy Spirit demagnetizing shower has been flowing along the pathways they traveled on to reach me and members of my family and family lines, dissolving all the negative energies before they could cause harm. Thank You, Holy Spirit!"

    b. Ask for forgiveness

Curses can be placed by wishing strongly for harm to come to somebody. Whether or not a person is aware of having placed curses against others, every curse they made in every lifetime that has not been cleared is a *karmic curse* hanging over them, their family, and their family lines.

Say: "Everybody this applies to, choosing with my will and speaking for this lifetime and all previous lifetimes of mine, I am sorry for having placed curses, hexes, or wishes for evil against you and your family, knowingly or unknowingly. I retract and cancel all those curses, hexes, and wishes for evil and ask you to please forgive me. Thank you!"

    c. Forgive others for placing curses against you:

"Choosing with my will, I forgive everybody who placed a curse or hex or wish for evil against me, my family, and family lines in this lifetime and all previous lifetimes of mine. May you find peace."

    d. Seal curses that are still in effect

"(In the name of Jesus), I seal all curses, hexes, and

other wishes for evil that are hanging over me, members of my family, and (or) family lines with triple spiritual lead. I seal all hypnotic suggestions and implants within my brain and the brains of members of my family and family lines with triple spiritual lead.

"(Holy Spirit), I ask for that protection to stay in place until it is no longer needed. Thank You!"

e. Clear hypnotic suggestions and implants

"Holy Spirit, please flow a demagnetizing shower through me and everyone in my family and family lines to dissolve hypnotic suggestions and implants. Please flow healing love through me and everyone in my family and family lines to heal any portions of our brains that they have damaged. Thank You!"

F. CLEAR SOUL TIES, REPRESSED EMOTIONS, VOWS

1. Cut Detrimental Soul Ties (6-12 Mo)

"I cut all soul ties between me and other people, Souls that are detrimental to me. (....), please clear and heal in me and in each of those people, Souls, whatever clearing and healing each of us needs. Thank You!"

2. Clear Carnal Soul Ties

a. Disavow, then take a shower

"I disavow receiving any more carnal satisfaction from the spirit of lust. Holy Spirit, please clear the spirit of lust from every part of my body, mind, and spirit. Also, please clear all carnal soul ties between me and other people (Souls). Thank You!"

While showering (bathing), say: "(....), I ask for a Holy Spirit Shower to flow through my body, mind, and spirit to wash the spirit of lust out of my system and fill me with the holiness of God. Thank You!"

    b. Clear with an egg

"A sexual contact with another person will always result in an astral connection [which] will remain for about a year with an ever decreasing intensity when the relationship is over in the physical plane. This connect.ion can be absorbed by [an] egg if you rub the genitals with it for the purpose of breaking the tie." (Mickaharic p. 60) Discard the egg.

3. Clear Umbilical Cords, Astral Connections (6-12 Mo)

    a. Ask the Holy Spirit

"(Holy Spirit), please place a protective valve that allows only love to travel in each direction in all spiritual umbilical cord connections between my Soul and other people (Souls) and between my Soul and Souls from my other lifetimes. Please thin out those connections and dissolve them when the time is right. Thank You!"

    b. Ask for help from your spirit guides and angels:

With a particular astral cord connection in mind, picture this: *"...unhook the cord with your right hand (releasing hand) and send it out of your aura or energy field. Ask your Highest Spirit Guides/Angels to help you remove it and send it/hook it back to the person it is connected to. Tell them you do not want the connection back, creating an energy shield from further connections."[5]*

4. Clear Balls of Repressed Emotions

    a. Release by use of imagination – Examples

To clear the ball of anger that was within me:
[| Picture a release valve at the top of where the anger is stored. Bless that anger. Inform it that it can begin escaping through that spiritual release valve, a small amount with each exhale of your breath. It is being enclosed in a protective shield each day as you ask for that around all negative energies.

Picture flexible bronze tubing from the release valve extending into a suitable area of the astral plane and a bronze spray head on the end of the tubing that transmutes the anger back to neutral energy.[1] |]

Thank You, Father God!

To clear the anxiety that was in my hip:

[| There is also a ball of anxiety in your right hip. Instead of commanding the anxiety to leave all at once (after having asked for protection and blessing the energy of anxiety), ask In-God-We-Trust Angels to take hold of the outer strand of the anxiety and pull it gently as other angels help rotate the ball of anxiety so the strand can continue unrolling.

Imagine that as God We Trust Angels carry the end of the strand into the astral plane, the fine strands of which it is composed sparkle a tiny bit and then disappear as they are converted back to the neutral energy they came from.

Allow the energy to be what it is at the moment. Then, invite it to be transmuted back to neutral energy. When love makes that invitation, the anxious, riled-up energy will gladly comply. You may ask for this process to begin as you sleep. Trust that the ball of anxiety will get cleared away.[1] |]

Thank You, Father God!

b. Release gradually through breath:

"All parts of me, please join in saying: 'Bless all you portions of my emotional body. Bless you, anger, anxiety, and other emotions bottled up within me. I invite you to gradually be released and transmuted back to neutral energy as I breathe peacefully in and out at set times during the day.'"

Father God suggested: For 1 or 2 days, each hour during the day, breathe in peace and love a few times, and breathe out fear and other pent-up emotions.

5. Cancel Detrimental Vows and Promises (6-12 Mo)

> Best said aloud. "Choosing with my will, I cancel all vows and promises that I made in this lifetime and in all other lifetimes that are detrimental to me and others.
>
> "(....), I ask for healing for myself and everyone else who needs healing in connection with the cancellation of those vows and promises. Thank You!"

6. Declaration of Being Divorced (Do Once)

> Say aloud to your former spouse (in spirit):
>
> "N__, I apply this to the moment our divorce became final and at this moment. 'I divorce you, N__. I declare that I am divorced from you. You and I are no longer married. I wish you well.'"

7. Declare That Prior Lifetime Vows Are Dissolved (Do Once)

a. Religious vows

> "Religious vows only apply while the person is living. I declare that in each lifetime that I was a nun, brother, or priest, the vow of obedience I made to the Mother Superior (Abbott) and the vows of poverty and chastity I made to God dissolved when I died. (....), I ask for healing for my Soul and the Soul of the Mother Superior (Abbot) in each of those lifetimes. Thank You!"

b. Marriage vows

> "My spouse in previous lifetimes, I am no longer married to you because death dissolves marriage vows. I cut all ties between my Soul and your Soul that are detrimental to me. I wish you well."

G. PRAYING PSALMS FOR CLEARING "SINS OF OUR FATHERS"

We recommend praying all of these Psalm portions for nine days. (Ref. HAT II pp. 337-338)

If you have never been married, open with:

"(....), I pray these psalms in the name of ancestors in my family lines and in my Soul line, including the ancestors of my in-laws, my spouse's in-laws, and my children's in-laws in other lifetimes of mine, back to the 4th generation and farther back if need be. Thank You!"

If you are or have been married, open with:

"(....), I pray these psalms in the name of ancestors in my family lines and N__'s (spouse's name) family lines, including the ancestors of my (our) in-laws and of my (our) children's in-laws, back to the 4th generation and farther back if need be.

1. Psalms of Affirmation and Petition

  a. ⁵Yes, my soul, find rest in God; my hope comes from him. ⁶Truly he is my rock and my salvation; he is my fortress, I will not be shaken. ⁷My salvation and my honor depend on God; he is my mighty rock, my refuge. (NIV Ps 62:5-7)

   ⁷I will praise the Lord, who counsels me; even at night my heart instructs me. ⁸I keep my eyes always on the Lord. With him at my right hand, I will not be shaken. ⁹Therefore my heart is glad and my tongue rejoices; my body also will rest secure, ¹⁰because you will not abandon me to the realm of the dead, nor will you let your faithful one see decay. ¹¹You make known to me the path of life; you will fill me with joy in your presence, with eternal pleasures at your right hand. (NIV Ps 16:7-11)

  b. ¹The Lord is my light and my salvation—whom shall I fear? The Lord is the stronghold of my life—of whom shall I be afraid? ³Though an army besiege me, my heart will not fear; though war break out against me, even then I will be confident. ⁴One thing I ask from the Lord, this only do I seek: that I may dwell in the house of the Lord all the days of my life, to gaze on the beauty of the Lord and to seek him in his temple.

⁵For in the day of trouble he will keep me safe in his dwelling; he will hide me in the shelter of his sacred tent and set me high upon a rock. ⁶Then my head will be exalted above the enemies who surround me; at his sacred tent I will sacrifice with shouts of joy; I will sing and make music to the Lord. (NIV Ps 27:1,3-6)

c. ¹To you, Lord, I call; you are my Rock, do not turn a deaf ear to me. For if you remain silent, I will be like those who go down to the pit. ²Hear my cry for mercy as I call to you for help, as I lift up my hands toward your Most Holy Place. ⁶Praise be to the Lord, for he has heard my cry for mercy. ⁷The Lord is my strength and my shield; my heart trusts in him, and he helps me. My heart leaps for joy, and with my song I praise him. (NIV Ps 28:1-2,6-7)

d. ¹⁵The eyes of all look to you, and you give them their food at the proper time. ¹⁶You open your hand and satisfy the desires of every living thing. ⁷The Lord is righteous in all his ways and faithful in all he does. ¹⁸The Lord is near to all who call on him, to all who call on him in truth. ¹⁹He fulfills the desires of those who fear him; he hears their cry and saves them. (NIV Ps 145:15-19)

e. ¹Praise the Lord. How good it is to sing praises to our God, how pleasant and fitting to praise him! ²The Lord builds up Jerusalem; he gathers the exiles of Israel. ³He heals the brokenhearted and binds up their wounds. ¹¹The Lord delights in those who fear him, who put their hope in his unfailing love. (NIV Ps 147:1-3,11)

2. Psalms of Praise and Thanksgiving

a. ¹I waited patiently for the Lord; he turned to me and heard my cry. ²He lifted me out of the slimy pit, out of the mud and mire; he set my feet on a rock and gave me a firm place to stand. ³He put a new song in my mouth, a hymn of praise to our God. Many will see and fear the Lord and put their trust in him. (NIV Ps 40:1-2)

b. ¹I love you, Lord, my strength. ²The Lord is my rock, my fortress and my deliverer; my God is my rock, in whom I take refuge, my shield and the horn of my salvation, my stronghold. ³I called to the Lord, who is worthy of praise, and I have been saved from my enemies. ⁴The cords of death entangled me; the torrents of destruction overwhelmed me. ⁵The cords of the grave coiled around me; the snares of death confronted me. ⁶In my distress I called to the Lord; I cried to my God for help. From his temple he heard my voice; my cry came before him, into his ears.

⁶He reached down from on high and took hold of me; he drew me out of deep waters. ¹⁷He rescued me from my powerful enemy, from my foes, who were too strong for me. ¹⁸They confronted me in the day of my disaster, but the Lord was my support. (NIV Ps 18:1-6, 16-18)

c. ¹I will exalt you, Lord, for you lifted me out of the depths and did not let my enemies gloat over me. ²Lord my God, I called to you for help, and you healed me. ³You, Lord, brought me up from the realm of the dead; you spared me from going down to the pit.

⁴Sing the praises of the Lord, you his faithful people; praise his holy name. ⁵For his anger lasts only a moment, but his favor lasts a lifetime; weeping may stay for the night, but rejoicing comes in the morning. ¹¹You turned my wailing into dancing; you removed my sackcloth and clothed me with joy, ¹²that my heart may sing your praises and not be silent. Lord my God, I will praise you forever. (NIV Ps 30:1-5, 11-12)

d. ⁵When hard pressed, I cried to the Lord; he brought me into a spacious place. ⁶The Lord is with me; I will not be afraid. What can mere mortals do to me? [7]The Lord is with me; he is my helper. I look in triumph on my enemies. [28]You are my God, and I will praise you; you are my God, and I will exalt you. [29]Give thanks to the Lord, for he is good; his love endures forever. (NIV Ps 118:5-7, 28-29)

e.   [4]I sought the Lord, and he answered me; he delivered me from all my fears. [5]Those who look to him are radiant; their faces are never covered with shame. [6]This poor man called, and the Lord heard him; he saved him out of all his troubles. [7]The angel of the Lord encamps around those who fear him, and he delivers them.

[8]Taste and see that the Lord is good; blessed is the one who takes refuge in him. [17]The righteous cry out, and the Lord hears them; he delivers them from all their troubles. [18]The Lord is close to the brokenhearted and saves those who are crushed in spirit. (NIV Ps 34:4-8, 17-18)

f.   [11]Teach me your way, Lord, that I may rely on your faithfulness; give me an undivided heart, that I may fear your name. [12]I will praise you, Lord my God, with all my heart; I will glorify your name forever. [13]For great is your love toward me; you have delivered me from the depths, from the realm of the dead. (NIV Ps 86:11-13)

g.   [1]I will give thanks to you, Lord, with all my heart; I will tell of all your wonderful deeds. [2]I will be glad and rejoice in you; I will sing the praises of your name, O Most High.[3]My enemies turn back; they stumble and perish before you. [9]The Lord is a refuge for the oppressed, a stronghold in times of trouble. [10]Those who know your name trust in you, for you, Lord, have never forsaken those who seek you. (NIV Ps 9:1-3, 9-10)

3. Psalms of Repentance

a. ¹Lord, do not rebuke me in your anger or discipline me in your wrath. ²Have mercy on me, Lord, for I am faint; heal me, Lord, for my bones are in agony. ³My soul is in deep anguish. Ho long, Lord, how long? ⁴Turn, Lord, and deliver me; save me because of your unfailing love. ⁵Among the dead no one proclaims your name. Who praises you from the grave?

⁶I am worn out from my groaning. All night long I flood my bed with weeping and drench my couch with tears. ⁷My eyes grow weak with sorrow; they fail because of all my foes. ⁹The Lord has heard my cry for mercy; the Lord accepts my prayer. (NIV Ps 6:1-7, 9)

b. ⁴Show me your ways, Lord, teach me your paths. ⁵Guide me in your truth and teach me, for you are God my Savior, and my hope is in you all day long. ⁶Remember, Lord, your great mercy and love, for they are from of old. ⁷Do not remember the sins of my youth and my rebellious ways; according to your love remember me, for you, Lord, are good.

¹¹For the sake of your name, Lord, forgive my iniquity, though it is great.¹⁶Turn to me and be gracious to me, for I am lonely and afflicted. ¹⁷Relieve the troubles of my heart and free me from my anguish. ¹⁸Look on my affliction and my distress and take away all my sins. ²⁰Guard my life and rescue me; do not let me be put to shame, for I take refuge in you. (NIV Ps 25:4-7, 11, 16-18, 20)

c. ¹Blessed is the one whose transgressions are forgiven, whose sins are covered. ²Blessed is the one whose sin the Lord does not count against them and in whose spirit is no deceit. ³When I kept silent, my bones wasted away through my groaning all day long. ⁴For day and night your hand was heavy on me; my strength was sapped as in the heat of summer. ⁵Then I acknowledged my sin to you and did not cover up my iniquity. I said, "I will confess my transgressions to the Lord." And you forgave the guilt of my sin. (NIV Ps 32:1-5)

d. ¹Lord, do not rebuke me in your anger or discipline me in your wrath. ²Your arrows have pierced me, and your hand has come down on me. ³Because of your wrath there is no health in my body; there is no soundness in my bones because of my sin. ⁴My guilt has overwhelmed me like a burden too heavy to bear.⁸I am feeble and utterly crushed; I groan in anguish of heart.

   ¹⁴I have become like one who does not hear, whose mouth can offer no reply. ¹⁸I confess my iniquity; I am troubled by my sin. ²⁰Those who repay my good with evil lodge accusations against me, though I seek only to do what is good. ²¹ Lord, do not forsake me; do not be far from me, my God. ²²Come quickly to help me, my Lord and my Savior. (NIV Ps 38:1, 3-4, 8, 14, 18, 20-22)

e. ¹¹Do not withhold your mercy from me, Lord; may your love and faithfulness always protect me. ¹²For troubles without number surround me; my sins have overtaken me, and I cannot see. They are more than the hairs of my head, and my heart fails within me. ¹³Be pleased to save me, Lord; come quickly, Lord, to help me. (NIV Ps 40:11-13)

f. ¹Have mercy on me, O God, according to your unfailing love; according to your great compassion blot out my transgressions. ²Wash away all my iniquity and cleanse me from my sin. ³For I know my transgressions, and my sin is always before me. ⁷Cleanse me with hyssop, and I will be clean; wash me, and I will be whiter than snow. ⁹Hide your face from my sins and blot out all my iniquity.

   ¹⁰Create in me a pure heart, O God, and renew a steadfast spirit within me. ¹¹Do not cast me from your presence or take your Holy Spirit from me. ¹²Restore to

me the joy of your salvation and grant me a willing spirit, to sustain me.

^{17}My sacrifice, O God, is a broken spirit; a broken and contrite heart you, God, will not despise. (NIV Ps 51:1-3, 7, 9-12, 17)

g. ^{8}Do not hold against us the sins of past generations; may your mercy come quickly to meet us, for we are in desperate need. ^{9}Help us, God our Savior, for the glory of your name; deliver us and forgive our sins for your name's sake. (NIV Ps 79:8-9)

h. ^{10}Some sat in darkness, in utter darkness, prisoners suffering in iron chains, ^{11}because they rebelled against God's commands and despised the plans of the Most High. ^{12}So he subjected them to bitter labor; they stumbled, and there was no one to help. ^{13}Then they cried to the Lord in their trouble, and he saved them from their distress. ^{14}He brought them out of darkness, the utter darkness, and broke away their chains.

^{20}He sent out his word and healed them; he rescued them from the grave. ^{21}Let them give thanks to the Lord for his unfailing love and his wonderful deeds for mankind. (NIV Ps 107:10-14, 20-21)

i. ^{1}Out of the depths I cry to you, Lord; ^{2} Lord, hear my voice. Let your ears be attentive to my cry for mercy. ^{3}If you, Lord, kept a record of sins, Lord, who could stand? ^{4}But with you there is forgiveness, so that we can, with reverence, serve you. ^{5}I wait for the Lord, my whole being waits, and in his word I put my hope. ^{7}Israel, put your hope in the Lord, for with the Lord is unfailing love and with him is full redemption. (NIV Ps 130:1-5, 7)

j. ^{1}May the Lord answer you when you are in distress; may the name of the God of Jacob protect you. ^{2}May he send you help from the sanctuary and grant you support from Zion. ^{3}May he remember all your sacrifices and accept your burnt offerings. (NIV Ps 20:1-3)

SECTION IV
PRAYERS FOR FAMILY LINES, SOUL LINE

A. DIRECTIONS

1. About the Names of the Family Lines (Soul Line)
   Clearing for One's (N__'s) Family Lines

   Substitute "**JOHN AND JANE DOE**" with your (N__'s) family name and "**SAM AND SUE SMITH**" with your (N__'s) spouse's family name.

   Clearing for One's Soul Line

   Substitute "the **JOHN AND JANE DOE** family line and the **SAM AND SUE SMITH** family line" with "my Soul line." Make changes as needed in the wording of the clearings and prayers.

2. Doing the Clearing and Praying

   Do numbers 9, Clear Negative Energies, and 10, Clear Outside Souls and Entities, on the same day, first 9, then 10. You may do the other steps in any order and spread them out over several days or weeks. Completing all of them will bring about the best results, but even doing some will do a lot of good for your family lines (Soul line).

3. Doing Clearing For Other People's Family Lines

   If you are doing a clearing for other people's family lines, invite them to join you while you are doing the clearing(s). If the people you will be doing a clearing for cannot join you, tell them the dates and times you will be doing the steps.

B. PRAYERS IN PREPARATION

Pray these prayers for nine days before clearing and healing your family lines. If you plan to do clearing and healing for another person's family lines, we suggest that both you and he (she, they) pray the prayers for nine days.

1. "(....), I lift to You everyone in the **JOHN AND JANE DOE** family line, my (N___'s) family line; and in the **SAM AND SUE SMITH** family line, my (his, her) spouse's family line, going back as many generations as necessary to bring about clearing and healing that is needed. Please touch each person and Soul in those family lines with Your grace to help enable them to forgive others so complete clearing of negative energies will occur.

2. "I ask all loving Souls in the **JOHN AND JANE DOE** family line and the **SAM AND SUE SMITH** family line, and all other loving Souls who are willing, to join in sending a barrage of blessings and love to (a) every person, Soul, and entity who took part in placing curses, hexes and other wishes for evil against me (N___) and members of my (his, her) family and family lines and to, (b) every person, Soul, and entity who took part in placing hypnotic suggestions or implants within me (N_) and members of my (his, her) family and family lines.

3. "I ask that a Holy Spirit demagnetizing shower will have been flowing along the pathways that those wishes for evil, hypnotic suggestions, and implants traveled on to reach me (N___) and members of my (his, her) family and family lines ever since those wishes for evil were put in place. Thank You, Holy Spirit!"

4. "Holy Spirit, please help me (N___), and everybody in my (his, her) family and family lines be truly sorry for having hurt others and be willing to forgive those that I am (they are) holding grievances against. Thank You!"

C. PRAYERS FOR CLEARING AND HEALING

Say these prayers aloud each time you go through clearing and healing processes for the family lines.

"Jesus, Lord Melchizedek; Archangels Michael, Haniel, and Zadkiel; and family members assigned to help clear these family lines, please assist us and surround us with love. We ask that each person, Soul, will be enabled to understand the prayers even though they speak (spoke) a different language. Thank You!

"We are here to do clearing for two family lines. We will first clarify that a "family line" is comprised of the person's parents, both birth and adoptive, and all current and former spouses of each parent; the person's grandparents and great-grandparents, and the spouses of each of those individuals going back to the beginning of their existence as a Soul.

"We are ready to begin. Members of the **JOHN AND JANE DOE** family line and the **SAM AND SUE SMITH** family line, please gather in spirit. Thank you!

"Before each prayer, I will say what the prayer is for and will invite you to join as I say it. I will say each prayer twice to give everyone a chance to join who wishes to.

Announce each prayer: "We will now..." then say the prayer.

1. Clear Erroneous Early Imprinting

    Please join: "I am worthy of being loved because I come from love. I *am* love. Father God, Mother God, the Holy Spirit, and Jesus love me! The universe loves me! All of them say that I am a beloved child of God! I join them in saying and proclaiming that I am a beloved child of God! I receive their love, and I love me!"

    "I am worthy of being loved because I come from love. I *am* love. Father God, Mother God, the Holy Spirit, and Jesus love me! The universe loves me! All of them say that I am a beloved child of God! I join them in saying and proclaiming that I am a beloved child of God! I receive their love, and I love me!" (2x)

2. Assist Unloving Souls to Become Loving

Please join: "Loving Souls in my (our) family lines and my Soul line, please join in flowing a deluge of blessings and love to every Soul in our family lines who is unloving because of painful circumstances during their lifetime or not having received enough love.

"Souls that are with people and Souls in my (our) family line and in my Soul line that are unloving because of painful circumstances during your life or not having received enough love, we flow a deluge of blessings and love to you. We invite you to receive the blessings and love and choose to become loving. Bless you!" (2x)

3. Release Painful Cellular Memories

Please join: *"Dear God, whatever my spirit mind and my cell memory might be holding from a past life that is harmful to me in any way, please help me release it into the cleansing white light of the Holy Spirit."* (Browne pp. 106-107) (2x)

4. Process of Forgiveness

a. Ask for forgiveness

I invite *every* person and Soul everywhere who wishes to ask members of the JOHN AND JANE DOE and SAM AND SUE SMITH family lines for forgiveness for something to join in this prayer. Family members who wish to ask for forgiveness, also, please join:

"Everybody in those family lines that this applies to, I am sorry for everything that I said, thought, did, or neglected to do that hurt you in any way. I am sorry for judging you and for placing curses, hexes, or wishes for evil against you and your family, whether without realizing it or on purpose. I retract and cancel all of them. Please forgive me." (2x)

b. Forgive others

I invite *every* person and Soul everywhere who wishes to forgive members of the **JOHN AND JANE DOE** and **SAM AND SUE SMITH** family lines for whatever it is to join in this prayer. Family members who wish to forgive others, please join in:

"Everybody in those family lines that this applies to, I forgive you for everything you said, thought, did, or neglected to do that hurt me in any way. I forgive you for any times you judged me or placed curses, hexes, or wishes for evil against my family and me." (2x)

c. Every person and Soul who asked others to forgive you, please join: "Thank you, everybody, for forgiving me! I am very grateful." (2x)

d. Every person and Soul who asked others to forgive them and everyone who forgave others, please join in saying an Affirmation of Forgiveness:

"I forgive others, and I forgive myself. God forgives me, and I am free."[2] (2x)

5. Protective Valve in Soul Ties and Umbilical Cords

Members of our family lines, please join: "Holy Spirit, please place a protective valve in all soul ties and spiritual umbilical cord connections between my Soul and other people (Souls) that allows only love to travel in each direction. Please thin out the umbilical cord connections and dissolve them when the time is right. Thank You!" (2x)

6. Cut Detrimental Soul Ties

Please join: "I cut all soul ties, including carnal soul ties, between me and other people and Souls in my family lines and in my Soul line that are detrimental to me. Holy Spirit, please clear and heal in me and in those other people (Souls) whatever clearing and healing each of us needs. Thank You!" (2x)

7. Cancel Detrimental Vows and Promises

Please join: "I cancel all vows and promises that I made that are detrimental to me and others. Holy Spirit, please heal me and everyone who needs healing in connection with canceling those vows and promises. Thank You!" (2x)

8. Declare That Prior Lifetime Vows Are Dissolved

Religious Vows:

Please join: "Religious vows only apply while a person is living. I declare in each lifetime in which I was a nun, brother, or priest, the vow of obedience I made to the Mother Superior (Abbott) and the vows of poverty and chastity I made to God dissolved when I died. Holy Spirit, I ask for healing for my Soul and the Soul of the Mother Superior (Abbot) in each of those lifetimes. Thank You!" (2x)

Marriage Vows:

Please join: "My spouse in previous lifetimes, I am longer married to you because death dissolves marriage vows. I cut all ties between my Soul and your Soul that are detrimental to me. I wish you well." (2x)

9. Clear Negative Energies

a. Clear enmeshment between negative energies and outside Souls

Please join: "(In the name of Jesus), I ask kindly and command each bit of negative energy that is with outside Souls and entities that are with me to release to each of those Souls and entities every portion of their being that is enmeshed with your energy. Thank you!

"Outside Souls and entities that are with me, please release every bit of negative energy that is enmeshed with your being back to the energy body it is a part of. Thank you!" (2x)

b. Clear enmeshment between negative energies and your Soul

Please join: "(In the name of Jesus), I ask kindly and command each of you bits of negative energy that are with me, to release to me every portion of my Soul that is enmeshed with your energy. Thank you!

"I release every bit of negative energy that is enmeshed with my Soul back to the energy body it is a part of." (2x)

c. Command the negative energies to leave

Please join: "I bless all energies that are with me. Any bit of that energy that chooses to become loving or neutral energy is now free to leave. Go in peace!

"(In the name of Jesus), I ask kindly and command all negative energies that are still with me to leave." (You: Cough)

"Holy Spirit, please transmute those negative energies back to their original form and return them to their proper dimension. Thank You!" (2x)

10. Clear Outside Souls and Entities

Please join: "Outside Souls that are not meant to be with me, please release to me all portions of my Soul that are enmeshed with your Soul. Thank you! I release to each of you all portions of your Soul that are enmeshed with my Soul that are not meant to be with me.

"In the name of Jesus, I ask kindly and command all outside Souls to leave that are not meant to be with me." (You: Cough)

"Angels, please guide those Souls to where they are meant to be. Thank you!" (2x)

11. Clear Supraphysical Shells

Please join: "Angels of the Violet Flame, please sweep violet transmuting flame through all supraphysical shells attached to my etheric body to dissolve them and transmute that energy into light. Thank you, angels!" (Starr pp. 102, 103 adapted) (2x)

12. Clear Contact Points For Negative Energies

Please join: "I ask for a Holy Spirit demagnetizing shower to flow through me to clear any contact points for negative energies that are present. Thank You!" (2x)

13. Clear Negative Thoughtforms

a. Clear astral cord connections to the thoughtforms

Please join: "Angels of the Violet Flame, please sweep violet transmuting flame through all negative thoughtforms that are attached to or hanging over me to dissolve the astral cords connecting the makers of those thoughtforms with my Soul and to dissolve the thoughtforms, transmute their energy, and release the energy to be used for good. Thank you, angels!" (Starr pp. 66, 98)

b. Clear enmeshment between the Souls and energies that are in the thoughtforms

Please join: "I seal with spiritual lead all negative energies in negative thoughtforms that a portion of my Soul is caught in.

"Holy Spirit, I ask for a demagnetizing shower to flow through those negative thoughtforms to clear stickiness so my Soul can separate from the negative energies more easily. Thank You!

"Negative energies in the negative thoughtforms (in the name of Jesus), I ask and command you to release every portion of my Soul that is enmeshed with your energy. Thank you! In turn, I release every bit of your energy and all portions of other Souls that are enmeshed with my Soul.

"By the sword of the Spirit, I declare that my Soul is separated from the negative energy and from all other Soul portions that are in the negative thoughtforms."

   c. Command the negative energies to leave:

> "I bless all energies that are with me (N___). Any bit of that energy that chooses to become loving or neutral energy is now free to leave. Go in peace!
>
> "(In the name of Jesus), I ask kindly and command all remaining negative energies to leave. (Cough)
>
> "Holy Spirit, please transmute those lower vibration (negative) energies back to their original form and return them to their proper dimension. Thank You!"

14. Clear Curses, Hypnotic Suggestions, and Implants

   a. Dissolve the roots of the curses and hexes:

> Please join: "Loving Souls in my family and family lines, please join in sending a barrage of blessings and love to every person, Soul, and entity who took part in placing curses, hexes, and other wishes for evil against me and members of my family and family lines.
>
> "I ask that ever since those curses, hexes, and wishes for evil were put in place, a Holy Spirit demagnetizing shower has been flowing along the pathways they traveled on to reach me and members of my family and family lines, dissolving all the negative energies before they could cause harm. Thank You, Holy Spirit!"

   b. Ask for forgiveness

> Please join: "Everybody this applies to. Choosing with my will and speaking for this lifetime and all previous lifetimes, I am sorry for having placed curses, hexes, or wishes for evil against you and your family, whether knowingly or unknowingly. I retract and cancel all of those curses, hexes, and wishes for evil and ask you to please forgive me. Thank you!
>
> "(....), please forgive me! Thank You!" (2x)

   c. Forgive others for placing curses against you

> Please join: "Choosing with my will, I forgive everybody who placed a curse, hex, or wish for evil

against me, my family, and family lines in this lifetime and in all previous lifetimes. May you find peace." (2x)

d. Seal curses that are still in effect

Please join: "In the name of Jesus, I seal all curses, hexes, and other wishes for evil that have not been cleared that are hanging over me, members of my family, and family lines with triple spiritual lead. I seal all hypnotic suggestions and implants that have not been cleared from within me and members of my family and family lines with triple spiritual lead.

"Holy Spirit, I ask for that protection to stay in place until it is no longer needed. Thank You!" (2x)

Please join: "Choosing with my will, I forgive everybody who placed a curse, hex, or wish for evil against me, my family and family lines in this lifetime and in all previous lifetimes. May you find peace." (2x)

e. Clear hypnotic suggestions and implants

Please join: "Holy Spirit, please flow a demagnetizing shower through me to dissolve all hypnotic suggestions and implants. Thank You! Please flow healing love through me to restore any damage that has been done by hypnotic suggestions and implants that have been within my brain. Thank You!" (2x)

15. Assist Souls to go to the light

"I place a positive vortex high up in the plane where the Souls are gathered that we have done clearing for that is to be used only for Souls to go to the light. Archangels and angels, please gather around the vortex as a welcoming presence.

"Jesus, angels, relatives, and friends of the Souls who are ready to go to the light, please be there to welcome them and accompany them as they go to the light. Thank you!

"I invite those Souls ready to do so to go to the light now. Bless you on your way! Thank you, Jesus, angels, relatives, and friends for welcoming and accompanying them as they go to the light!" (2x)

D. CLOSING PRAYER

Please join: "Thank You, Father-Mother God, Holy Spirit, for the healing and clearing that took place for members of the **JOHN AND JANE DOE** and **SAM AND SUE SMITH** family lines.

"Please seal all negative energies that are still with people (Souls) in those families and that are hanging over family members and our family lines with triple spiritual lead. Please flow peace and love into every person (Soul). We entrust ourselves to Your care. Thank You!" (2x)

APPENDIX

A. COPPER RINGS (TENSOR RINGS, QUANTUM RINGS)

HOW THEY CLEAR NEGATIVE ENERGIES

"Within a Tensor is an infinite source of energy that is neither electric nor magnetic. Its output is beneficial and healing to all life forms. It is a superconductor. It neutralizes magnetic fields. It brings coherency to chaos, and it produces a measureable gravitational effect... Tensor Rings were conceived by the late Slim Spurling, a world famous geo-dowser with an interest in metaphysics and a vision of planetary healing. ...

"Slim knew that linear objects have polarity. He found evidence for it in trees and in a length of wire. Playing with this concept, Slim formed a closed loop that resulted in an electromagnetic column of energy emitted perpendicular to the enclosed loop. 'Beneficial' energy was produced on one side of the loop while 'nonbeneficial' energy was produced on the other. To alleviate the negative effects, Slim folded the wire in half and then twisted it before joining the ends together. Viola! The Tensor was born. [Heavier gauge wire makes the tensor field stronger.]

"Slim later discovered that John Archibald Wheeler had done extensive work with closed loop coils. Wheeler called the field created by the loop a 'tensor field.'"[6]

"Although short-term use of tensor rings on the body can be beneficial, their long-term use in one place is not recommended. For this reason it is not recommended that they be worn as bracelets or pendants, or over the head for a long period of time."[7]

BENEFITS OF TENSOR RING TECHNOLOGY (partial list)

1. "When the ring is put under the bed, it effectively neutralizes negative fields of geo-pathic origin. [Definition below]
2. "The ring can also be utilized to increase meditative state.
3. "It can effectively clean an aura when slowly lowered from the head going down to the foot and reachies the back part of the body.
4. "It can mend bones in a faster way.
5. "It can potentate (perfectly energize, purify) water by setting the bottle over the tensor ring.
6. "It can keep the swimming pool clean by placing the ring at the pump.
7. "It can also be used in a showerhead.
8. "It also relieves joint pains.
9. "Ideal for well-being and overall health.
10. "It reduces stress.
11. "Effective relief from mental as well as physical pain.
12. "It enhances the healing process during illness or injury.
13. "It decreases stress due to EMFs [electromagnetic radiation from electronic devices]
14. "Increase plant growth"[8]

> geopathic *adj.* 1 relating to the theory that natural irregularities in the earth's magnetic field can be intensified by power lines, underground pipelines, and other natural and man-made features such that a stress field harmful to human health and well-being is created (en.wicktionary.org/wiki)

Approximate Diameter of Tensor Rings

1 Cubit 7" 3/4 Cubit 5.25" 1/2 Cubit 3.50" 1/4 Cubit: 1.75"

Where to Purchase Tensor Rings

twistedsage.com tensorsmith.com dancingwithwater.com lightlifetechnology.com mariediamond.com Amazon

B. SENSITIVES

SENSITIVES: ARE THEY REAL?

"The term 'sensitives' is used to refer to people who are thought to have an increased sensitivity to paranormal or spiritual energy, which allows them to perceive or experience things beyond the realm of normal human experience. Sensitives are sometimes also referred to as 'Psychic sensitives,' 'psychic empaths,' or simply 'empaths.' The term is often used to describe people who are able to sense the presence of spirits, ghosts, or entities, or to describe people who are able to pick up on the motions, thoughts, or experiences of others, even at a distance.

"Some of the traits and abilities that are associated with sensitives include having a strong intuition and the ability to sense things that others cannot, being highly empathetic and able to pick up on the emotions and feelings of others and to understand their experiences in a deep and meaningful way...

"The field of psychology and neuroscience provides evidence of the existence of empathy, intuition, and other well-documented human abilities that can contribute to the perception of heightened sensitivity to emotional or spiritual energy. However, the idea of a 'sensitive' as a person with paranormal abilities is not supported by mainstream science and is often considered to be part of the realm of pseudoscience or paranormal beliefs."

(www.higgypop.com/news/sensitive-are-they-real/)

More information: "The Differences Between Empaths and Highly Sensitive People" drjudithorloff.com

C. ALPHABETICAL LIST OF PRAYERS AND CLEARINGS

Roman numerals II and III refer to sections.
See Contents for the page numbers.

GENERAL

Addiction, Ask for Help to Overcome – II.D.8
Apply, Reapply Prayers – II.D.4
Ask Angels for Protection II B.5
Ask for a New Gatekeeper – II.D.1
Ask for a Spiritual Ministry Team to Be Assigned – II.D.2
Ask for Protective Valve in Soul Ties, Umbilical Cords – II.B.9
Ask to Be Ministered to In a Healing Ring – II.C.3
Ask to Be Ministered to in Heaven Hospital – II.D.3
Call on Angels of the Violet Flame – III.C.4.b
Cancel Detrimental Vows and Promises – III.F.5
Cancel Judgments You Made Against Others – II.E.1.a
Clear Balls of Repressed Emotions – III.F.4
Clear by Use of Imagination – III.A.8
Clear Erroneous Early Imprinting – II.C.7
Clear Karma (Process of Forgiveness) – II.E
Clear Objects, One's Home, Buildings, Areas – III.A
Clear with Bowl of Water, Ice Cubes III.A.7
Clear with Lit Candle, Holy Water III.A.6
Clearing for Animals – III.D.2
Clearing for Plants – III.D.1
Clearing, Prayers for – II.C.3-4
Compress of Spiritual Vinegar – III.C.4
Create a Spiritual Copper Ring – III.A.5
Declare That Prior Lifetime Vows Are Dissolved – III.F.7
Declaration of Being Divorced – III.F.6
Fill food with Divine love – II.A.5
Full Body Prayer – II.D.13
Grounding Exercises – II.C.1
Healing Touch: Smooth Out Aura, Clear Neg. Energies – II.D.11
Help Alleviate Medical Conditions – II.D.7

NEGATIVE ENERGIES

Clear Enmeshment: Neg. Energies-Your (N's) Soul III.B.1.c
Clear Hypnotic Implants – III.E.5
Clear Incorporation of Energies Retroactively – III.B.1.a
Clear Negative Energies from Self, Others – III.B.1.a-d
Clear Negative Thoughtforms – III.E.3
Electronics: Protection from Negative Energies II.B.6.c
Names: Protection from Negative Energies – II.B.6.b
Photos: Protection from Negative Energies – II.B.6.a
Send Negative Energies into a Negative Vortex – III.A.12

SOULS

Assist Souls to Go to the Light (Inc. Animals) – II.D.15
Assist Unloving Souls to Become Loving – II.D.16
Clear Carnal Soul Ties – III.F.2
Clear Enmeshment: Outside Souls, Your Soul – III.C.1.b
Clear Lying Spirits, Mischievous Spirits – III.C.3
Clear Soul and Energy Residue – II.D.5
Clear Soul Enmeshment of Outside Souls – III.C.1.b
Clear Soul Incorporation by Nine-Day Process – III.C.1.e
Clear Soul Incorporation Retroactively III.C.1.a
Clear Soul Infestation – III.C.2.a-g
Clear Supraphysical Shells – III.C.4
Clear Umbilical Cords, Astral Connections – III.F.3
Clear Unwanted Outside Souls from Self, Others – III.C.1.a-c
Create a Positive Vortex for Souls to go to Light – II.D.14
Cut Detrimental Soul Ties – III.F.1
Separate Mother's Intergrafted Soul from Yours – III.C.6
Separate Siamese Twin Soul from Your (N's) Soul – III.C.5
Soul Retrieval – II.D.14

BIBLIOGRAPHY

Bodine, Echo, *Echoes of the Soul* c 1999, New World Library, Novato CA

Browne, Sylvia, *A Psychic's Guide to Our World and Beyond,* c Sylvia Browne 1999, Signet (New American Library, division of Penguin Putnam Inc. Penguin Books Ltd.)

Emmanuel's Book: A manual for living comfortably in the cosmos, compiled by Pat Rodegast and Judith Stanton, c 1989 Bantam Hover-Kramer, Dorothea, *Healing Touch: A Guidebook for Practitioners,* c 2001, Cengage Learning

Freeman, James D, *Prayer of Protection,* Written in 1940-1941 as a prayer for protection during World War II, a prayer promoted by Unity School of Christianity

HAT I, Leigh, Lorrie, *Healing Across Time I,* c 2023, iUniverse

HAT II, Leigh, Lorrie, *Healing Across Time II,* c 2023, iUniverse

ISV International Standard Version, Bible Gateway, www.biblegateway. com. Accessed Nov 2023

Mickaharic, Draja, *Spiritual Cleansing: A Handbook of Psychic Protection,* c 1982, Samuel Weiser, Inc.

NIV New International Version, Bible Gateway, www.biblegateway. com. Accessed Aug 2023.

Right Use of Will: Healing and Evolving the Emotional Body, c 2010. Ceanne DeRohan. Four Winds Publications

Starr, Aloa, *Prisoners of Earth: Psychic Possession and Its Release,* c 1987 by Aloa Starr, 2nd Edition, c 1993, Light Technology

Unity School of Christianity, Affirmation of Protection

Webster's New World College Dictionary Fourth Edition, c. 2004, Wiley Publishing, Inc., Cleveland, Ohio

Wright, Machaelle Small, *MAP: The Co-Creative White Brotherhood Medical Assistance Program,* c 2006, Perelandra, Ltd

GLOSSARY

Disclaimer: I make no representation or warranty of any kind, express or implied, as to the accuracy of the non-referenced definitions given below. The understanding of spiritual realities is constantly evolving, and scientific and psychological research is ongoing. Lorrie Leigh

astral cord – an energy connection "made of astral and etheric energy [that] connect[s] two people's subtle bodies"[9]

aura – the four energy bodies surrounding the human body taken as a whole: the etheric, emotional, mental, and spiritual bodies. Pictures of auras are obtained using Kirlian photography.

balm of Gilead – 1 *a)* a small evergreen tree of the bursera family native in Asia and Africa *b)* the resinous juice of this tree, used in ancient times in an aromatic ointment (Web p. 111)

by intention – choosing for something to take place and believing that it will, somewhat picturing it in one's imagination

cellular memory – "Body memory (BM) is a hypothesis that the body itself is capable of storing memories, as opposed to only the brain. ...there are currently no known means by which tissues other than the brain would be capable of storing memories. ...it has become relevant in treatment for PTSD." (Wikipedia)

"Modern science teaches us that our cells contain DNA which is the blueprint for the complete design of our physical bodies. They also hold the blueprint for our emotional, mental and spiritual state. Our cells remember all of who we have been in past lives and all that has been in this life right up to the present day (hence the term cellular memory). So as we change and grow in any aspect of our lives, our cells are constantly updating our personal data. Cells also retain the information of all life experiences that has been absorbed from genetic heritage, nothing ever experienced whether positive or negative escapes being programmed."[10]

charismatic prayer meeting – a gathering to praise God, receive instruction, spend time in silence, and pray for others, usually with gifts of the Spirit in evidence, including praying in tongues

clearing – removing outside Souls and entities that are not meant to be with a person; removing negative, dark energies

contact point for negative energy – THIS WRITING: a connecting point for negative energy that is attached to or implanted within a person's body or aura that attracts similar energies; created and put in place by another person's (Soul's) intention or by use of witchcraft energies

copper ring (tensor ring) – See Appendix A

copper ring, spiritual – THIS WRITING: an invisible copper ring created by intention, the effectiveness of which lasts about 24 hours.

curse – *n.* 1. a calling on God or the gods to send evil or injury down on some person or thing (Web p. 356)

curse, karmic – a curse that is hanging over someone and their family as a result of that person or a family member having placed that curse on someone during their current lifetime or a previous one

dark energy center – THIS WRITING: an energy-seeking center that has dark (negative) energies mixed in with Soul portions[2]

demon – an energized evil thoughtform

energy-seeking center – THIS WRITING: a cluster of small portions of Souls that need clearing and healing that are magnetically attached to another Soul to receive healing

entity – *n.* 1 being; existence 2 a thing that has definite, individual existence outside or within the mind... (Web 475) THIS WRITING: human Soul, animal soul, thoughtform, demon (see definition), fallen angel (Lucifer and angels that followed him)

erroneous early imprinting – THIS WRITING: the belief, picked up early on in the Soul's existence, that they are not worthy of being loved

family distress – THIS WRITING: physical and emotional symptoms triggered within a person when loved ones and/or people (Souls) in their family lines or Soul line experience distress family lines – THIS WRITING: a person's and their spouse's birth and adoptive parents, grandparents, and great-grandparents (and spouses) going back to the beginning of their existence as Souls

Full Soul – THIS WRITING: the portion of a person's original Soul that is with God plus all portions of it that are currently living lifetimes, are with other people, in the astral plane, in Heaven, or elsewhere. Each portion of a Full Soul lives a human life only once.[2]

gatekeeper – an elemental (spiritual entity) which guards the psychic door at the base of the skull (Starr pp. 44, 51)

go to the light – a Soul going to its right place: Heaven or elsewhere

hex – a magic spell, a curse (Oxford Dictionary, online)

healing ring – THIS WRITING: a ring of love and light surrounding a Soul; a ring of love and light that we can ask to have surround ourselves (others) to be ministered to by angels[2]

healing touch – doing clearing and healing from within a person's aura (Hover-Kramer pp. 109-110)

Heaven Hospital – THIS WRITING: a hospital in Heaven for Souls described by Echo Bodine where people can be ministered to while still living (Bodine pp. 49-50)

help Souls become loving – extend much love and blessings for a period of time to Souls that are unloving due to difficult circumstances in their life

Higher Self – THIS WRITING: one's Full Soul[2]

Holy Spirit demagnetizing shower – THIS WRITING: A flow of spiritual energy from the Holy Spirit that loosens the magnetic attraction between a Soul and negative energy and Soul residue

Home Soul – THIS WRITING: a person's Soul in their current lifetime

implant – "a controlling device, generally of astral substance... implanted by psychic means [or] hypnosis." (Starr pp. 67, 74) A hypnotic suggestion could be implanted.

In-God-We-Trust Angels – a band of Angels one can call on to come with a net of golden light to carry entities away (Starr pp. 8, 28, 165)

in spirit – speaking to a person without them being present

incorporation – see Soul incorporation

karma – Buddhism, Hinduism: the principle of cause and effect where an individual's intent and actions cause (influence) their future (Wikipedia) mantra – a word or sound repeated to aid concentration in meditation, such as "Om; Ohm" (the "sound of the universe")[11]

Medical Assistance Team (MAT) – a heavenly ministry team that is a function of "the Great Brotherhood of Light...The Sisterhood of Light...an organization of Ascended Masters, Angels, and Cosmic Beings united for the highest Service to God...includes Jesus the Christ, Gautama Buddha, Mother Teresa...Archangel Michael"[12]

Mighty Astrea – one of the Elohim {angels) of the seven rays[13]

negative energy – THIS WRITING: For each person, energy that has a lower vibration rate than their energy; energy that is lacking in positive character, such as anger or greed; energy that diminishes, deprives, or denies a person's energy; negative spirit

outside Soul – THIS WRITING: any Soul that is not a part of the person's Soul in their current lifetime; an outside entity

place for visiting Souls – THIS WRITING: one of several planes of existence located within a person's aura

poltergeists – "mischievous entities who delight in playing pranks... knock on the walls or furniture, hide things only to have them suddenly reappear, and cause many other...problems" (Starr p. 96)

residue, energy – "tiny particles that got separated from the mass of energy that either float in the air or cling to people, animals or objects by static attraction"[2]

residue, Soul – small bits of the astral body of Souls that are separated from the Souls they are a part of

right place for unloving Souls – THIS WRITING: Home for unloving Souls

saffron – II. dried, aromatic stigmas [of certain species of iris] used in flavoring and coloring foods...formerly in medicine (Web p. 1262)

shade – THIS WRITING: a portion of the astral body of a Soul

Siamese identical twin Soul – THIS WRITING: the Soul of a person's identical twin that is still connected to the person's Soul because the Soul did not divide completely when the embryo divided

Siamese fraternal twin Soul – the incorporated and enmeshed Soul of the person's fraternal twin that did not survive

Soul enmeshment – THIS WRITING: portions of Souls being mixed together

Soul incorporation – THIS WRITING: portions of an outside Soul that are enmeshed with a person's Soul being within some of the cells in that person's body, helping to sustain life

Soul infestation Type One – a portion of an outside loving Soul intermingling with a baby's Soul at conception or shortly afterward

Soul infestation Type Two – a portion of an unloving Soul intermingling with a baby's Soul at conception or shortly afterward

Soul infestation Type Three – negative energy intermingling with a baby's Soul at conception or shortly afterward

Soul line – THIS WRITING: A person's Souls from all previous lifetimes

Soul retrieval – assisting separated portions of Souls to return to the Soul they are a part of

soul tie – a spiritual/emotional connection between people

soul tie, carnal – a soul tie between people that is an aspect of the spirit of lust[2]

Soul, unloving – 1. A Soul that came forth unloving II. A Soul that became unloving due to experiencing painful life circumstances.

Souls, intergrafted – THIS WRITING: A mother's protectiveness for herself can extend into her baby and somewhat "glue" a portion of her child's Soul to her Soul, creating a pathway between them. (HAT II pp. 31-32)

supraphysical shell – calcified matter or shell attached to the astral body that was formed from "a habit, fear, or emotional behavior pattern that has been deeply imprinted in the etheric body" (Starr p. 102). It can be from a current or previous lifetime.

the salvation of Souls – THIS WRITING: Souls going from a place of fear to a place of love; being saved from fear and hopelessness

thoughtform – an energetic construct, floating vibration of energy, created every time words are spoken, or thoughts are thought; they attach to or hang over people who have similar energies; they can be beneficial or nonbeneficial (synthesis of definitions offered by several schools of thought). THIS WRITING: Tiny portions of the Souls of those who spoke those words or thought those thoughts are attached to the thoughtform. See demon.

transmute – to change from one form, species, condition, nature or substance into another; transform; convert (Web p. 1522) umbilical cord, spiritual – one type of astral cord

"...the coalesced spiritual energy of love, mercy, justice, freedom, and transmutation."[14] Angels who work with Archangel Zadkiel are called Angels of the Violet Flame.[15]

unloving Soul – THIS WRITING: A Soul that came forth unloving or that became unloving due to painful life circumstances. "Father God says in *Right Use of Will* that there are Spirits of Loving Essence that thrive on love and Spirits that are not of Loving Essence that seek 'reduction in consciousness, compression, and death.' He says every Spirit has the right to be in the place that feels right for them. Loving Spirits and unloving Spirits are not meant to be together. Unloving Spirits were allowed to enter the Earth by people having sex without love." Right pp. 42, 50 (HAT II p. 22)

vortex, negative – an area in which energy spirals counterclockwise, downward

vortex, positive – an area where energy spirals clockwise, upward

OTHER BOOKS IN THE SET

HEALING ACROSS TIME I
Healing for Parts and all of Me

HEALING ACROSS TIME II
A. Between My Souls and Other Souls
B. For Our Family Lines

REFERENCES

1   https://www.nia.nih.gov/health/end-life/providing-care-and-comfort-end-life
2   www.okrehab.org/substance-abuse/addiction-feelings-disease/
3   Portion of a lesson received from Spirit
4   *Unity's Daily Word.* publishing date unknown
5   www.themystica.com/skinny-astral-cords Dana Cribari
6   www.scribd.com/document/137645168/ Besco twistedsage.com
7   dancingwithwater.com
8   photonorgone.co.uk/what-are-tensor-rings-26-w.asp
9   www.alchemyrealm.com/cords.htm
10 naturalhealthcourses.com/2015/06/cellular-memory-and-how-it-works/
11 www.onetribeapparel.com?... OM-symbol-meaning
12 www.Ascension-Research.org
13 www.ascension-research.org/astrea.html
14 www.violetflame.com/the-secret-of-the-violet-flame/
15 Who Is Archangel Zadkiel? Angel of the Violet Flame (ask-angels.com)